PRAISE FOR *PERFECT IMBALANCE* AND UMESH MANATHKAR

"Umesh has a deep understanding of the semiconductor business, in addition to the technical skills you would expect of a large public company CIO. It's a great combination, and why I've hired him twice into public company CIO roles. For aspiring CIOs, Umesh's book is a 'must read.'"

— **Steve Kelley**, President & CEO, Amkor Technology

"I had the privilege of working side by side with Umesh for many years. *Perfect Imbalance* is a distillation of his experiences in business and IT. It is a great volume for CEOs and business people who manage IT functions or want to understand how to get maximum value from this function in today's digital economy."

— **Dan Artusi**, Semiconductor Executive and Board Member

"I have been working for Broadcom for the last twenty-five years in IT, which has evolved from HP to Agilent to Avago to Broadcom, so I can vouch that IT is more than technology. It's all about taking risks and changing the culture to increase the business value while reducing the cost. *Perfect Imbalance* cleverly defines the dynamics among these factors. It's a vital book for all IT professionals to deliver business outcomes that matter."

— **Andy Nallappan**, VP and CIO, Broadcom Inc.

"With technology becoming the focus of almost every company, CIOs must approach their roles as business leaders first, technologists second. In his highly readable, very pragmatic book, Umesh Manathkar lays out a framework for innovation, cost containment, and risk mitigation that allows all CIOs to deliver maximum value to their businesses."

— **Martha Heller**, CEO of Heller Search Associates, and author of
Be the Business: CIOs in the New Era of IT

"One central theme of Umesh's book is that a CIO must understand the company's business first, thoroughly and completely, before relying on IT technical knowledge. Instead, many IT professionals may believe their skills are generally transferable, across multiple industries and business models. But the truly effective CIO, or for that matter CFO, General Counsel, VP, HR person, and the like is one who knows their company's market, product, technology, and customers so well that they can apply their functional expertise in a uniquely business-specific manner."

— **Bill Bock**, Board Director and Advisor

"Moving from IT Manager to CIO is no small feat, and Umesh Manathkar has succeeded at this. His lessons learned and explained in *Perfect Imbalance* are unique and compelling and can only be told by someone who has experienced them. Change needs to be purpose-driven, and you can only define the real purpose when you become the Business Partner, not just the CEO and CFO, to the entire organization. Umesh's focus on being a Business Partner has helped him see into the organization to lead the change that adds value."

— **John Kurtzweil**, Director at Pallidus, Inc., Finance Executive and Advisor

---

"*Perfect Imbalance* is an invaluable resource that provides powerful guidance for IT leaders unable to communicate the real business value they create. With smart and practical tools, you'll learn how to get unstuck discussing budgets, and instead, how to put your energy into the valuable contributions you make to the organization."

— **Susan Friedmann**, CSP and International Bestselling Author of
Riches in Niches: How to Make it BIG in a small market

"I highly recommend Umesh Manathkar's *Perfect Imbalance* to everyone within IT, regardless of their level or role. The importance of balancing IT's value, cost, and risk through the proper business-oriented CIO lens is the essence of successful IT leadership. This book is also a must read for CEOs who want to maximize the return on their IT investment."

— **Eric Bloom**, Executive Director, IT Management and Leadership Institute

Perfect Imbalance

The Key To Enabling Business-Centric IT

Umesh Manathkar

AVIVA
PUBLISHING
New York

Perfect Imbalance: The Key to Enabling Business-Centric IT

Published by:

Aviva Publishing
Lake Placid, NY, USA
(515) 523-1320
www.AvivaPubs.com

Umesh Manathkar
Email:info@perfect-imbalance.com
Phone: (480) 567 5333
perfect-imbalance.com

ISBN: 978-1-950241-09-5
Library of Congress Control Number:2019905845

Editors: Tyler Tichelaar and Larry Alexander, Superior Book Productions
Cover and Interior Book Design: Meredith Lindsay

Every attempt has been made to source properly all quotes.
Printed in the United States of America

Perfect Imbalance

The Key To Enabling Business-Centric IT

Umesh Manathkar

AVIVA
PUBLISHING
New York

To my parents, and my loving family to whom I am forever grateful.

Acknowledgments

This book is a compilation of what I have learned over the last twenty-five years in Information Technology (IT). I wouldn't have had the luxury of sharing my experiences had it not been for the many great opportunities I have had in my career. I consider myself very lucky for having had the chance to enjoy such an enriching career.

None of this would have been possible had it not been for the many well-wishers, mentors, and coaches I've had in my professional career. Many of them gave me opportunities and challenges that I could have only dreamed of. There are many people to thank, but I would like to mention a few who have made a big difference in my career. I thank Daniel Artusi for trusting me with a CIO role in a public company for the first time. Dan had the courage to recognize that the effective CIO would be someone who understands business processes and automation, not just someone with a traditional IT background. That big first step set me up for a successful career as a CIO over the next twenty years. Another big personality in my career is Bill Bock. Bill was my biggest supporter early in my career and has been my mentor ever since. I learned a great many things from Bill about what sets successful leaders apart from the rest of the crowd. I also want to thank John Kurtzweil for giving me challenging roles and advice over the last few years. Finally, I can't thank Steve Kelley enough for trusting me with big responsibilities at two different companies over the last twelve years. Steve continues to be my biggest supporter and mentor to this day and someone I admire a lot. I still continue to learn a great deal by observing his leadership skills. I am forever grateful for knowing and having the opportunity to work with all of them.

No professional life can be successful without an enriched personal life. I am grateful to my dad and mom for the many great personal sacrifices they made to ensure my success. I am also grateful to my wife Smita for our long friendship and love and for being the anchor of our family. I am grateful to my children, Rohan and Ria, for their unconditional love and support, no matter what. I am amazed every day by how much I learn from my children and their knowledge and opinions in wide ranging areas. My family members are my best supporters in the whole world.

I also want to thank several people who helped me immensely with publishing this book. Eric Bloom has given timely advice and continued support throughout this journey. Martha Heller shared her experience of publishing books and made the process much easier for me. I want to thank Susan Friedmann for agreeing to publish this book, Tyler Tichelaar and Larry Alexander for their great help in editing, and Meredith Lindsay for designing the book cover and interior layout. All of them helped transform my manuscript into a publishing-worthy book. Thank you all for helping me reach this stage. It wouldn't have been possible without your expertise.

Finally, I want to thank all my business and industry peers, my fellow CIOs in my professional network, industry experts, and my professional associates over the past twenty-five years, from whom I've learned so much. Kevin Haskew has been very kind to lend his support by writing the foreword for this book. Such an endorsement from a successful fellow CIO peer means a lot to me. I dedicate this book to all the IT professionals who are working hard every day to make a difference and who aspire to become Chief Information Officers (CIO) one day. If I can do it, I am sure you can too.

Contents

PART V: WHAT DOES IT TAKE TO DELIVER THE "PERFECT IMBALANCE"?

Lead the IT team to achieve the highest **Business Value** with the least **Cost** without taking undue **Risks**.... Yes, that's possible.

Foreword

The CIO's role is constantly changing, and a lot has been written about having a business focus and being value driven. However, not many practical lessons have been published from successful CIOs for the best ways to become a business-centric, value-driven, successful CIO. Every CIO knows that demand is always greater than supply. They also realize more ways exist to solve the same problems today than were available before. This situation is further complicated by the fast pace of technological evolutions leading to new solutions, vendor hype, and the democratization of IT. These strategic shifts happening in the IT industry have substantially changed the demands on the CIO and the CIO's role.

What is needed to be a successful CIO today is vastly different from what was needed just ten years ago, yet some fundamental rules of this role have never changed. Those fundamental rules define the key responsibility of every CIO: to ensure their business runs smoothly day-in and day-out; i.e., operational excellence and understanding the organizational culture and capability. From this understanding, you can build credibility and a strategic roadmap map for how to move forward, including adoption of new technological trends and solutions. I see many CIOs forgetting their primary responsibilities and then wondering why they are losing their credibility. In today's confusing world of competing solutions and conflicting priorities, it's easy to go after a new hype or shiny object and forget the primary responsibility. Conversely, a CIO cannot just focus on the present and not modernize or attempt to satisfy the pent-up demand from internal customers. With the democratization of IT, a CIO cannot control all aspects of IT but needs to provide guidance, leadership, and a framework for the organization to work within. The challenge today is that a CIO has to make sense of all of these competing forces.

Perfect Imbalance is a very good depiction of the real challenges every CIO faces and the practical approach to deal with these challenges. This book outlines the concepts and methods necessary to balance the business value and risks in a systematic way. That balance is the key to achieving long-term and sustainable success for any IT team and organization.

Umesh brings his long standing experience to plot this path to help show future CIOs what it takes to manage this perfect imbalance. He offers a pragmatic perspective from somebody who has been doing this for many years and figured out what it takes to both survive and thrive in this challenging role of a twenty-first century CIO.

A book like this has great value for people who really want to know what it takes to be successful. It is essential reading for somebody aspiring to become a CIO, but also a good sanity check for seasoned practitioners. I strongly recommend this book to all IT professionals.

Kevin A. Haskew
SVP & CIO, ON Semiconductor

Introduction

This book is dedicated to all IT professionals who are working hard to make a difference and who aspire to one day becoming a top-level Information Technology executive. I was inspired to write this book because, over my long career, so many young colleagues have come to me for career advice. In all such conversations, the gist of all their questions is simple: What does it take to become a CIO (Chief Information Officer)? And, more importantly, how can I get there? In a nutshell, they are seeking all the essential building blocks they should focus on right now. They want to know behind-the-scenes journey details to get to that top spot.

As simple as these questions are, I've often found myself answering them with long explanations and stories about CIO roles and responsibilities. I also found out that the answers to these questions are not that straightforward. They may require a much broader understanding of the role, the company, one's background, and many similar factors. Over the course of a few years, I realized many misconceptions exist about CIOs even among IT professionals.

Another thing I realized in all my conversations is that most answers are related to things I never learned in academia. I spent more than ten years in college earning my engineering and business degrees, but none of my studies taught me what I found myself sharing with my aspiring colleagues.

Most of the advice I gave centered around first explaining what the CIO role is, and more specifically, what it's not. Then I built on the key aspects of the responsibilities the CIO role entails. CIOs are IT executives primarily focused on delivering business value to an organization through information technology solutions. While that's the mission of this role, understanding what constitutes business value and how to deliver it is what often makes or breaks people in this role.

It is also a bit surprising to many IT professionals to realize how business-heavy this job is. It's a more technical and specialized job than general management, but it's not 100 percent technical. A solid dose of business acumen is a prerequisite for the successful CIO. That non-technical component of the role is where most of the failures occur.

In addition to both technical and business leadership, a key specialized skill is required to be a successful CIO—the ability to manage seemingly conflicting needs to continuously deliver higher value at a lower cost while constantly monitoring and mitigating risks. That's the *perfect imbalance* a CIO is expected to achieve and the key to real success.

I wrote this book to include many of my lessons learned over twenty-five years in the IT industry, close to twenty of which have been as head of IT for several public corporations. This book is based on my successes and failures in dealing with a wide variety of IT problems over the course of my career. It provides a different perspective on the CIO's role and outlines how to become a proficient leader in information technology.

This book is best looked upon as a handbook for all IT professionals in a corporate setting. However, although it's written as a guide for aspiring CIOs and focuses on larger companies with C-suite executive structures, its framework is useful to most IT professionals in their current roles. It provides essential insights into all the non-technical and leadership aspects of the journey to that top spot in the IT department.

I hope you find this information useful, and I wish you much good fortune as you launch or continue to pursue your IT career.

Sincerely,

Umesh Manathkar

Part I

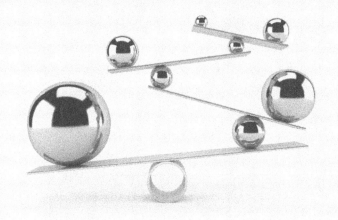

The Role of a CIO

CHAPTER 1

The Role of a Chief Information Officer

What does a CIO do?

Chief Information Officer (CIO) or head of Information Technology (IT) is a crucial role for any large organization in any industry. The role is very similar in any corporate organization. The IT department provides the technological backbone for all functions of a company. In today's world, every task performed by every team member can be traced back to a technological function. In addition, information technology is the most common catalyst for significantly improving performance across all industries.

For the sake of discussion, we will use CIO to refer to whoever oversees information technology in an organization. All organizations need and have someone acting as CIO. Whether you are in healthcare, hospitality, travel, manufacturing, journalism, or any other industry, you need someone to take care of your information technology needs. It's not always a formal position, but if you are responsible for your company's information technology, you are basically a CIO. However, this book is about becoming an actual CIO, a title that applies to companies with complex organizational charts and distinct departments, so we will focus on these larger corporations; thus, the language used will reflect the needs of all *complex organizations*. As such, when you read "All companies need/have blank," understand that your local, independently-owned convenience store or the independent plumber you call when a pipe breaks doesn't have the same needs or organizational structure as the companies we are focused on in this book.

What exactly does a CIO really do? A CIO is typically responsible for managing all computing hardware and software systems, collectively called Information Technology. Every company needs some software applications and hardware to run its business. For example, applications used by all its employees—email, intranets, internal social media, office productivity suites, file systems, cloud apps, chat applications, etc. All users also need necessary computing hardware such as desktops or laptops, cell phones, printers, etc. All the companies also need many back-office systems to run behind-the-scenes operations for the company. Such systems include: order management applications, billing and invoicing systems, financial/bookkeeping systems, inventory tracking systems, warehousing and manufacturing execution systems, research and development systems, etc. Every company also needs some customer engagement systems (front office systems), such as an ecommerce site, website, customer relationship management (CRM) system, quoting system, order management system, etc.

To run all these software systems, companies need a lot of hardware, such as servers, storage devices (enterprise grade hard disks), networking devices to link all these users and systems, wireless network systems, phone systems, etc. Many of these hardware units come in industrial form and can be stacked in specially designed racks. All those racks are housed in a specially designed facility called a data center. These data centers have special cooling and heating systems as well as extra protection from power outages—usually with expensive, uninterrupted power supplies (UPS) or generators.

For most companies, data centers are their nerve centers. Every user is virtually interacting with that data center every moment without even knowing it. A small blip in that nerve center affects the user's productivity or other mission-critical functions. For example, in high volume manufacturing, a short outage in the execution system can affect the day's production and hence significantly affect revenue. Not to mention the nightmare that follows when trying to restore customer confidence in your manufacturing or shipping operation.

Many newer software applications are Cloud-based. The Cloud is a metaphor used to explain the new business model where IT resources are hosted and managed in someone else's (the Cloud Provider's) data center. It started being referred to as the Cloud to indicate that you, as a customer, don't need to worry about it. It's taken care of by someone else. We will discuss this Cloud phenomenon in detail in other sections of the book.

To manage all this software and hardware, whether on your premises or in the Cloud, you need experienced IT professionals who specialize in these technologies. The CIO is typically a leader of all the teams collectively managing these hardware and software systems. Given the complexity of all the technologies involved, a great deal of specialization is required. Every IT department typically has anywhere between twenty to thirty IT specialty roles, based on areas of expertise and levels of experience.

Most IT teams are organized into four sub-teams, responsible for hardware, software, customer service, and administration. Hardware teams include roles such as systems administrators, storage administrators, network administrators, and security administrators. Software teams include positions such as Enterprise Architect, Business Analyst, Functional Analyst, Software Developer, Systems Administrator, Tester, and Project Manager. Customer service teams typically include IT helpdesk associates and applications help desk associates. Other IT administrative functions include project managers, business liaisons, program managers, vendor management, and asset management.

The value of information technology can vary from being necessary for business survival to being a catalyst for business growth. Given IT's stature and significance, most companies have sizable IT teams and considerable IT budgets. Also given the value of IT, the head of this organization, the CIO, is typically considered to be among the top executives in a company.

CIOs usually report to either the CEO, CFO, or COO, but are considered independent heads of IT department and have full responsibility and accountability for delivering IT value.

Above is a simple description of an IT department and the CIO role. This is how many CIO job descriptions are written. However, this does not explain the real role or the challenges associated with this role. If the CIO role was merely about managing technology, then you wouldn't see the variations in the levels of expertise, compensation, reporting structure, and responsibility scope from one company to another. You wouldn't see many failures either. All the CIOs would be stellar success stories. However, that's not the case. Many succeed and an equal number fail in this role. This role has unique challenges that rival the difficulties in many other functional leadership roles. For this reason, I would argue that CIO is one of the riskiest positions in any company. You will see why that may be the case in the next few chapters.

CHAPTER 2

What's the Real Role?

It's never written in any job description

However fundamental and value-adding the CIO role is, it is often very complicated to explain. It varies considerably based on the company's nature, the complexity of business operations, and the level of sophistication the business needs to excel in the marketplace. The CIO role is similar in some ways, yet it can also be very different from company to company.

The tactics, mission, and use of technology may differ from company to company; however, there are some fundamental principles common to this role in any company of any size in any industry.

One way to explain a CIO's role is as we discussed above—as someone responsible for managing all the hardware and software and the teams responsible for IT. However, that is a straightforward explanation that does not explain what's really expected. It does describe the role of a CIO at the most basic level, which we all know is generally just the tip of the iceberg in almost any role. For someone who has to fully comprehend what it takes to deliver all those IT services and what's involved behind the scenes, or to understand what it takes to stay ahead in the game continuously, this is just a starting point—something you can write in a job description.

When interviewing for a new CIO, no one is looking for just a good team leader or someone who knows information technology. They are implicitly looking for something much more critical to the company's success and someone who can deliver it for them—someone who has all the ingredients and a track record of getting things done and upping company performance.

The CIO's role can be very simply summed up as someone responsible for applying *information technology to maximize business value at the least possible cost while mitigating the risks.* The catch here is to understand what the business value is. It differs from company to company.

Simply put, the CIO must understand which tasks and projects belong to which of the three key success factors—business value, cost, and risk management. The CIO also needs to understand the interplay between these three factors and how it affects the success of IT teams and, ultimately, the company's success or failure. That is something that must be continually in front of you and always balanced.

Although every task you execute falls into one of these three categories, no tasks or projects are ever labeled accordingly. You may be working on a hundred different activities, but it's your job to know whether a task fits into any of these three factors or is irrelevant. One can make an argument that if you are working on something that does not fall into one of these three categories, it must be irrelevant, and you should seriously consider ignoring or eliminating it.

So, how do you determine the interplay and the correct level of focus among these three key areas? For that, you first need to understand your CEO's mission for the company. If you can't make the connection between your work and your CEO's mission, you will be an IT leader who "doesn't understand the business." Overcoming this is the first critical step in "business-IT alignment." If you, as a CIO, can't connect the dots between IT work and business success, how can you expect your team to align with the business' mission?

When looked at in detail, the IT mission for one company could be very different from that for another. For example, a small start-up's IT mission could be survival, just getting to that very first big order, while IT in another small, yet established company could be hyper-growth in a particular market. The IT mission for an old, established company could be about enhancing the value of well-established products and technology. Some companies could be working on compliance issues or cybersecurity, and that may very well be IT's primary mission for the foreseeable future. For some companies, the mission could be very specific and narrowly defined, while for others, it may be defined broadly and with long-term intent.

IT's focus is unique to your company's needs. Based on the life stage of a company and what its short-term priorities are, the company's mission could be drastically different. That pretty much dictates the role and mission of IT and the CIO.

I was once approached for a CIO role at a company where they defined the CIO's mission as the successful implementation of an enterprise resource planning (ERP) system. That's all they wanted from their new CIO. At another company, they explained the CIO's success or failure was tied to getting security under control. I know several industry peers who were hired by companies for their expertise and track record in managing compliance risks, while other factors were less important based on the mission of that particular company at that time.

If you are good at only one of the three ingredients—business value, cost, and risk—you cannot deliver the full package for a company. What each company needs is the right combination of the three factors. That right combination is the highest value, *lowest* cost, and correct level of risk mitigation. Tactical goals for any company may very well focus on any one of the three components, but over the long term, good results are expected in all three areas. Moreover, only a true CIO with the right management and leadership skills can succeed in this long-term journey.

To do proper justice to this role, a fourth essential ingredient that sets success apart from failure is needed—specialized leadership skills in managing IT. While very simple when articulated at this high level, what sets apart a successful CIO from a not so successful one is figuring out

ways to create the highest level of value at the least possible cost by appropriately managing the risks. This seems like a great imbalance because
conventional wisdom would tell us that to deliver higher value and lower
risk, you would have to spend more money. However, the real challenge
for any CIO is to accomplish this imbalance.

The art to being a CIO is in mastering this imbalance perfectly. Any of
these three components can easily take over, commanding your full attention and bogging you down completely. However, if one takes over, it
will lead to incorrect or less than perfect imbalance. I have seen many
IT departments in heavily regulated industries where risk management is
the primary function and very little time is left to manage costs or value
equations.

Another factor that can drastically change IT's mission is the scope of
service desired. I often classify IT services in different tiers: bronze, silver,
gold, and platinum levels. Bronze level IT service may include only the
essential functions, with basic technology and lots of risks acceptable to
business owners. The silver level could be better in technology, sophistication, risk management, response times, etc. At the top end of the spectrum, platinum IT service may be at the forefront of business innovation
and growth using the best technology. Platinum level IT not only delivers
all the essential functions well, but it is also often the catalyst in advanc-
ing the business itself.

The cost associated with platinum IT service is much different from the
cost of bronze and the results vary widely as well. Unless you understand
and can explain the difference to business owners, they may demand platinum IT at bronze prices. In one business, IT could be the utility provider that merely keeps old systems running, while in another, IT could allow
the company to become a leader in their industry.

While IT's mission is different from one company to another, the fundamental framework for figuring out the right level of IT is pretty much the
same. The insights we will discuss here will be useful in any IT department, of any size, at any stage in a company's life, in any industry.

Reflecting what we have just gone over in some detail, this book is organized into four major sections covering these vital aspects of the CIO role.

- Maximize Value
- Minimize Cost
- Manage Risk
- Master IT Leadership Skills

The insights in this book came from my personal experience working in IT for the last twenty-five years and in the role of CIO for fifteen of those years. This book is not an in-depth technical reference on any one aspect of IT, but a collection of the concepts that worked or did not work for me. I fully expect many to agree, and just as many to disagree, with the opinions discussed in this book, as no two CIOs are the same. Everybody uses their own wisdom in their own ways to support their company's success.

This book neither asserts that these are the only best practices nor claims to be the sole authority on these topics, but I can certainly vouch from my personal experience that collectively, all the insights discussed here are good ingredients for what makes IT successful. I wish I had known these things fifteen years ago when I started as a CIO of a then small company.

CHAPTER 3

State of IT

Where do we currently stand?

Understanding that Value, Cost, and Risk are the three major pillars of IT management. It's wise first to gauge exactly where we stand in these three major areas. To start with, here is a quick, high-level assessment tool for understanding where a company stands in each of these areas.

Many IT management consultants and CIOs have a great deal of expertise in assessing the current state of IT and proposing course corrections. Many of them also use a very sound framework and structured methodology to evaluate the state of IT in great detail. That kind of assessment may be useful, especially if you need a major turnaround or a reset. However, a simple checklist-based assessment as discussed below is a good starting point. This kind of assessment allows one to determine where one needs to put extra energy.

Given this simple way to explore each of these threads, this assessment is a very simple and easy to use tool. By design, it's a very high-level qualitative and subjective assessment. We don't want to make it a very granular or very structured assessment at this stage so that we can ensure the high-level view is correct.

You can assess the current state of IT along these ten dimensions using whatever scale you prefer, but a simple range of one to five, with one being the worst and five being the best, can do the magic.

Category	Score (1-5)
BUSINESS VALUE	
1. Digital transformation *The extent to which all business processes are automated or at least digitized.*	
2. End customer value added *How involved are IT systems in all customer engagement processes from end to end? Do systems drive all aspects of customer engagement—front and back-end included?*	
3. Business KPI *How well is IT driving the company's success on its key performance indicators, both quantitative and qualitative, whatever they may be—revenue, cost, profit, market share, product launch, cycle time, yield, customer satisfaction, renewals, etc.*	
4. Technology sync *How well have you kept up with modern technologies? Mobile, Cloud, IoT, virtualization, Big Data, Analytics, Blockchain, multimedia collaboration, if applicable?*	
5. Keeping the Lights On (KTLO) *How well are you ensuring near 100 percent availability of all current IT systems? Are they operating with little to no business interruption?*	
RISK	
6. Statutory compliance *Is the company in full compliance with all regulatory, legal requirements worldwide? IT has a role to play in compliance in all areas of the company.*	
7. Disaster protection and business continuity *What is the state of IT systems for disaster protection and business continuity? A company must be able to perform its business operations through most disasters. IT systems are the most critical part of that risk management.*	

Category	Score (1-5)
8. Cybersecurity *By far the most significant risk area for most companies. Do you have a sound cybersecurity program that focuses on prevention, deterrence, monitoring, education, and active incident response to manage all types of cyber threats?*	
IT COST	
9. Competitive cost structure *Is your IT spending in line with your competitors or industry peers?*	
10. Flexible cost structure *Is your IT cost structure flexible enough to absorb shocks during bad years without any adverse long-term effects?*	

Table 3-1: State of IT Assessment

The purpose of this assessment is to understand key areas of focus. As such, you are not shooting for a certain total score. The total score does not really matter. What matters is whether you have a qualified level of competency in each of these factors.

What you are looking for in this assessment is that we are at least good or very good (at least four) in each of these dimensions, no exceptions. If we are below four, then we need to focus on improving in that area.

This may seem pale compared to the structured and detailed assessments many IT consulting companies provide that may be hundreds of pages long. However, this has proven to be a very successful starting point for me in understanding strengths and weaknesses quickly. It is also useful in communicating with key stakeholders in straightforward language.

This book is dedicated to exploring these three critical areas in detail. That discussion is then complemented by a description of the essential skills CIOs must possess to deliver this *perfect imbalance* between delivering the highest value at the lowest cost while managing the risks precisely.

Part II

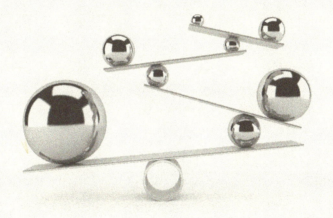

The Value Equation

CHAPTER 4

What Is IT Value?

And why does it matter?

Value is by far the most discussed word in the IT world. Every conference or CIO meeting I have ever attended has always discussed some variant of the business value provided by IT. At times, IT's value seems very abstract. It's vague. It's not something straightforward and easy to grasp. There, indeed, aren't many prescriptive ways for measuring and delivering IT value. Everyone defines it differently. However, everyone in IT agrees that value is by far the most critical success factor for any IT department.

Most CIOs I know are constantly being challenged to demonstrate the value of IT to their company. IT has to continually prove its worth. This demand comes from the fact that everyone uses information technology in one way or another to do their job. That is the best aspect of IT. It is probably the only function in any company that touches all the functions, all users, at all times. IT is involved at tactical as well as strategic levels everywhere. IT is crucial not only for doing routine tasks but is often a catalyst for enhancing performance throughout the organization.

Throughout my career as a CIO, I have seen many strategic roadmaps and vision statements for various departments. All those departments cite extensive use of information technology as a critical success factor. Very few functions can improve their performance without using technology. Every department periodically goes through strategic deep-dive discussions and comes out with a long list of tactical and strategic priorities.

Many, if not most, of those priorities and projects depend on use of current or enhanced technology. That's where value enters the picture. IT services are a commodity used by everyone all the time and are desperately needed to progress further. No one will ever deny that IT brings value to the table. Otherwise, IT departments would have vanished a long time ago. What you see now is precisely the opposite. You see IT budgets flourishing and team sizes growing. That's because people comprehend the value delivered by IT. However, what everyone differs on is whether IT has met their expectations and helped them accomplish all their technological ambitions. That's where you will see a wide variation in opinions.

Value is the most critical and intriguing factor for IT. Nothing else matters if you, as a CIO, don't get the value equation right. It is of the utmost importance, but it also happens to be complicated and very difficult to define—it's very ambiguous. It mostly depends upon the subjective assessments of others. Assessments based on data and metrics exist, but many times the assessments are subjective, based on "gut feelings." There are very few metrics for measuring the value IT brings. Moreover, the metrics that do exist differ from one company to another or even from one person to another in the same company.

However complex and ambiguous this value factor may be, no CIOs will ever deny that this is, by far, the most crucial factor for the IT team's success, and therefore, the success of the company itself. CIOs are continually striving to understand business value and deliver it every hour of every day. Moreover, most CIOs I know do an outstanding job enhancing the value the IT department brings to the table.

Here are some of the difficulties involved in assessing IT's business value:

- It's ambiguous and poorly defined at best.
- It's subjective and changes from one person to another.
- It's inconsistent and differs from one company to another, one industry to another.
- It's a moving target with the definition of value changing from time to time.

- It's rarely objectively assessed, as objective criteria and metrics exist only for a portion of the value equation and they don't matter as much as the subjective criteria.
- It's often in conflict with other value factors.
- It's hit or miss as to whether or not it aligns with the company's overall mission.

However challenging, complex, ambiguous, and fluid the concept of value is, if you, as a CIO, want to be successful, you must have a deep understanding of the value IT brings to your company. In the next few sections, we will try to get our arms around defining this value.

Objective value

There is a portion of value that can be defined objectively with the help of standard metrics—some direct and some indirect metrics help us judge the value created by IT. The value determined by the company's performance metrics is an indirect value. This may include financial or non-financial metrics that are important to the company's mission. Such metrics are specific to a company at a given point.

These metrics include:

- Revenue
- Granularly defined revenue—by geography, store, country, region, division
- Gross margin
- Profit
- Selling, general, and administrative costs
- Research and development cost
- Market share
- Product launch
- Initial public offering
- Customer satisfaction scores

These are not direct IT metrics, but they are often tightly connected to IT value. CIOs are expected to focus IT energy to support such performance metrics directly or indirectly. IT resources are often used in driving one or more of these performance indicators. Moreover, while there may not be a direct link, most people understand that IT plays a vital role in driving such business performance.

Then there are metrics specific to IT's performance that are considered direct value metrics. Standard metrics shed some light on the value factor important to any company. Standard metrics include:

- **Service level agreements (SLAs)**—define expected service levels.
- **Availability of systems**—measured in percent of uptime, sometimes excluding planned downtime while sometimes including it.
- **Number of major incidents**—based on service outage or performance threshold, which could be poor performance even if a system is not down completely.
- **Service outages (frequency, duration, resolution time)**—especially for mission-critical systems.
- **Customer service metrics**—include SLAs for response and resolution times, measuring how long it takes to respond to and resolve an issue based on priority with priority levels having different thresholds.
- **Customer satisfaction scores**—subjective scores gathered from surveys.
- **IT cost**—measures performance against budget or expected IT spending.
- **Headcount**—measures how many direct or indirect (contract) employees are in IT.
- **IT cost as a percent of revenue**—another standard IT cost metric.

The above standard IT metrics shed some light on IT's value. These metrics may get us one step closer to articulating IT value, but not by much. I have not seen these metrics satisfy stakeholders often. Most stakeholders can't relate to these metrics. CIOs often show their performance based on these metrics but rarely get applause for doing a superb job—except maybe for a cost metric.

IT's business value is easier to perceive when we show performance against other sets of metrics that stakeholders can relate to. Unfortunately, no standard metrics exist in this category. These metrics are connected to the company's mission, and everyone can relate to them. For example, if a company's mission is to reach a billion dollars in revenue in three years, one measure that could directly connect IT value to that mission would be the change in the sales team's productivity measured as revenue per salesperson after implementation of new technology.

Here are just a few examples of such metrics that I have seen making an excellent connection between IT effort and the value it delivers. There are dozens more, and they differ from one company to another, but the following list provides an idea of such metrics:

- Percent of process automation
- Level of digitization
- Percent of paper-based vs. paperless processes
- Productivity index—revenue per employee, shipments per employee
- Product or service quality index—number of returns
- Time to market
- Return on assets
- Financial close cycle time
- Manufacturing yield, cycle time, throughput, use
- Shipping accuracy
- On-Time delivery performance
- End customer satisfaction score
- Customer experience index

These metrics are often used by IT stakeholders (internal customers) for demonstrating their own performance. They make an excellent example of the value IT brings to the table, as perceived and expressed in their own language. These are also the metrics that make it to senior management and the board because they are an excellent proxy for the company's ultimate mission goals.

Any connection that CIOs can demonstrate between IT effort and business performance along these metrics is a step in defining and articulating IT value. However, these objective metrics show only a portion of the value IT delivers. Objective value as demonstrated by such metrics is necessary but not enough to prove the full value of IT. What really matters is the subjective value.

Subjective value

The good news is that everyone in a company interacts with IT. The bad news is that everyone interacts differently and has a different set of expectations. Sure, everyone has different needs. Subjective value brings the ambiguity we discussed earlier. It's value from the perspective of a "consumer" of IT services. However complex and fluid the subjective value is, it supersedes objective value defined by metrics. You cannot ignore it just because it's not easy to grasp.

All key stakeholders—CEO, CFO, other C-suite executives, the board of directors, functional or geography heads—want something different from IT. And they decide whether IT is adding value based solely on their perspective. Understanding key stakeholders and their expectations is crucial for delivering value. In some cases, expectations overlap, while in others, they may conflict. In many instances, they are unique to an individual—which makes it very difficult to succeed in everyone's eyes.

Apart from key, top-level stakeholders, there are also large communities that perceive IT value differently. Here are some of the principal communities:

- End users
- Functional users of departmental systems
- End customers (real customers of the company)

- Board of directors/audit committees
- Internal and external auditors
- Suppliers
- Partners (distributors, procurement partners)

These are very important communities that depend on information technology. Then there are still other communities that also have a perception of IT systems, albeit indirectly:

- The public at large (interacting with your website and similar public facing technology).
- Potential future customers/partners.
- New candidates exploring opportunities at your company.

All these stakeholders and communities have very different expectations of IT and define IT's value differently. Many times, I have within the span of one day received a message from someone about a great job one of the IT associates did and another message about how frustrated they are with a system, infrastructure, or even another IT associate. Such a scenario is prevalent in the IT world because IT services are very broad and deep and touch everyone.

Internal vs. external value

Many IT departments focus on internal IT value, the value delivered to other departments, IT's internal customers. They focus on the things that matter in running the business and all the systems used by internal customers. Truly transformative IT departments go a step beyond and focus on external IT value as well. That is the value perceived and realized by the end customer.

Most IT roadmaps are dominated by demands from other business functions, partly driven by their respective roadmaps. However, very rarely do you see a roadmap from your customers for their needs. That's your CEO's job, and from the technology perspective, your job as a CIO. If IT is focused only on internal demands and remains a step removed from understanding end customers, it is an internally relevant IT department, at best. Being internally relevant only is okay, but it does not tap into IT's real potential for making significant contributions to a company.

The real focus for CIOs should be going beyond internal customers who present themselves as a proxy for the end customer. CIOs who understand end customers, the market, industry, and competition, and who figure out how technology can play a role in setting their company apart from the rest will win in the long run.

It's not easy for CIOs to interact with end customers directly because others perceive IT solely as an internal function. While that is important, the real potential lies in understanding external value.

CIOs who understand external value from the end customer's perspective and what they need will automatically drive the internal customers to align with their goals. In many cases, understanding value from the end customer's perspective allows CIOs and IT associates to deliver something even better and quicker.

Given such ambiguity, complexity, and breadth of expectations, how should CIOs focus on value? Which IT services, stakeholders, or communities do they focus on? Moreover, what aspects of services do they focus on?

Unfortunately, the answer to all these questions is "all of them." However, the real skill of a CIO is to cut through the noise and focus on the correct aspects of IT value. CIOs need to understand what aspects of IT value matter to the company's mission. That understanding is clear only if there is a strong "IT-business alignment." With proper business alignment and the right people and correct priorities, CIOs can partner with everyone to deliver a custom portfolio of value that makes sense for a given company.

In the next two chapters, we will discuss the people aspect of the IT value equation and ways to lock in IT-business alignment. Those two factors are crucial building blocks for delivering IT value.

CHAPTER 5

Who Determines IT Value?

Know the stakeholders and their expectations

If the subjective value is far more critical than the objective value, then we better focus more energy on that. The key to understanding subjective value is to first understand the stakeholders who assess IT's value. In other words, who are the consumers and sponsors of IT services and what's their value perspective?

There are several roles in each company that assess IT value and would be direct about what they expect and how they value IT. There are also large communities who passively evaluate IT value but may not provide feedback directly. CIOs need to understand such passive consumers and address their value perceptions as well.

The one big difference today compared to IT in the 1980s and '90s is that everyone is a lot more knowledgeable about information technology. Thanks to the consumerization of information technology, IT knowledge is not confined to only a few technical workers in the company. Everyone acts as CIO of their household, and most are now familiar with concepts like networks, wireless routers, applications (app), operating system (OS), bandwidth, hardware, software, memory, data storage, network printers, cloud drives, and so on. Not too long ago, these were arcane and techni-cal terms to most people. Today, not only are people familiar with these terms, but they are also skilled enough to tinker with them and do some basic troubleshooting.

Today's end users also have some of the most advanced and user-friendly technology at their disposal, making them a lot more efficient. Sure enough, they are now extrapolating that experience and expect and demand similar things when they walk into their offices. They also see technology as a catalyst offering lots of opportunities to improve and streamline their business processes. That translates into an eagerness for getting their technology problems solved by IT as quickly as possible, without too much hassle.

Everyone consuming IT services is a good thing, both at an individual and functional level. Individuals and teams have diverse IT needs, goals, and expectations, but there are several common perceptions and expectations among all IT stakeholders. Understanding these expectations is very important to solving this value puzzle. Stakeholders, end users, team members—whatever you call your internal customers, they all have certain perceptions and expectations. Here are the primary themes:

- IT systems should run behind the scene 24/7 without a hitch and at all locations. IT systems are essential services like utilities. Proudly, IT has lived up to these expectations for the most part.
- IT can and should do a lot more to help team members in all departments with automation.
- IT holds the key to achieving their full potential.
- IT has to be fast enough to help them with their projects. Solutions need to be available at the speed of thought or, in some cases, before anyone even has the thought.
- IT teams don't seem to understand "business." Ironically, IT is probably the only organization that has a 360-degree view of the company because they work with everyone. However, there is some truth to this idea that IT folks don't understand business processes. We will discuss this more in the IT-business alignment section.
- IT should be given more resources and money because it can help the company in a big way.

- IT systems are often thought of as being inferior to competitors. This is unlikely in most cases, but it's a perception CIOs must be prepared for.
- IT systems lack sophistication, which is a primary cause of whatever performance issues the company is facing.
- IT enterprise systems are inferior and less user-friendly than consumer technologies. This, unfortunately, is a fact. Consumer technologies are way ahead of enterprise systems for a multitude of reasons.
- IT alone is responsible for cybersecurity. Users seldom understand the role they play in curbing the problem.

Above and beyond these generic expectations, all departments and users have specific, yet very diverse needs. In the next section, we will very briefly discuss a few familiar roles in any organization, their priorities, and their expectations of IT. The purpose here is not to discuss each stakeholder's role in detail but to focus on their needs and expectations from IT. Although I discuss specific roles below, I will not be discussing their individual needs but more of the entire functions or departments they lead. You will see that the expectations have a broad spectrum that CIOs need to address to make everyone happy. Meeting all these different expectations to the fullest is another crucial aspect of achieving the perfect imbalance.

Specific Roles

Chief executive officer (CEO)

CEOs prioritize meeting short- and long-term financial goals promised to investors and the Board of Directors. They also strive to ensure that all key performance indicators such as profitable growth, market share, and new products are delivered successfully. CEOs also focus on executing their strategic vision for the company.

In my personal experience, most CEOs have very reasonable expectations of IT. I have had the fortune to work with several admirable CEOs, and they all demonstrated very balanced expectations. They want to make sure there are no operations interruptions so all aspects of the organization can continue to do their work. They certainly don't want any hindrance to meeting quarterly or annual financial goals. They want to ensure the organization is compliant with regulations. They want their company operations to be fully secure.

Besides these day-to-day expectations, they also want IT and CIOs to bring technology solutions to the table that can advance their strategic agenda. This, in itself, is the most challenging task for most CIOs.

Chief financial officer (CFO)

The CFO's key priorities are relatively consistent across all countries and industries. Their goal is to contain costs and thereby improve profitability, ensure timely and accurate accounting, ensure statutory compliance for reporting, manage risk areas, and ensure cash management.

To perform their primary responsibility of financial accounting for the company, they depend a lot on IT teams and systems. Finance teams are one of the major user-bases for IT departments. Here is what CFOs generally expect from IT: Assurance that enterprise resource planning (ERP) systems operate continuously without any hiccups, help with all projects that lower costs, and support for the monthly, quarterly, and annual financial accounting closure (called the Close) and regulatory/tax compliance.

If CIOs report to CFOs, then there is unique dynamics, both for CFOs and CIOs. Most CFOs recognize that IT is a corporate function and not just another department under their leadership. Such CFOs allow CIOs to focus evenly across all functions in a company, depending upon the need and not focus exclusively on accounting functions.

I have seen most CFOs rise well above accounting function, especially if they have exposure to non-accounting functions. Their perspectives and expectations are much more aligned with those of CEOs and are in balance with the larger business picture.

Board of directors / audit committee / internal & external auditors

The Board of Directors is responsible for the company's overall governance and guides management in strategic decision making. The full board does not usually get involved with IT or have deep expectations beyond believing IT should be an integral part of company operations.

The board's audit committee, however, is focused on risk management. Lately, the most critical risk factor has been cybersecurity. Before this, audit committees were focused only on regulatory compliance, disaster recovery, and business continuity, from an IT risk point of view. Their expectations of IT are that we are investing enough energy mitigating these risk factors while remaining in compliance with applicable regulations. Of all the reports I have presented, over 80 percent have focused on cybersecurity. Given an audit committee's focus on risk management, all other aspects of IT are subordinate to monitoring and mitigating risk factors. They also want to hear from CIOs that CIOs are being provided sufficient leeway, resources, and funding to address those risks.

In all public companies, internal and external auditors are considered an extended arm of the board's audit committee. They focus on monitoring all the risks, especially regulatory compliance risks, in detail, providing a level of confidence for the audit committee and, therefore, investors at large. Audit teams focus on IT from a compliance or risk perspective. They have a laser focus on regulations and want to ensure that those are addressed adequately. Although other risks, such as cyber risk or business continuity risk are not driven by regulations, auditors do provide their guidance on what's expected from the shareholder's perspective.

It is essential that auditors have information about all IT controls, risks, and mitigation strategies, and CIOs must ensure that auditors get complete and accurate information. That allows auditors to gauge the level of risk and form an opinion that can be relayed to the CEO and the audit committee. Their confidence in IT's ability to handle risks is essential and should not be underestimated.

Business unit general managers / line of business heads

General managers (GMs) are the most influential and important group of business leaders. They are responsible for the bulk of the profit and loss (P&L) effort by product line. They are focused on all aspects of the business, including customer engagement, product marketing, and new product introduction. They are the ones who sign off on revenue targets along with sales executives. They are in many ways mini-CEOs for their portion of the product portfolio.

Despite being among the most influential and critical stakeholders, their expectations of IT are reasonable and light in nature. I have never had any tough conversations with this group of folks, unlike many other functions. That is also mostly because their teams aren't involved with the bulk of transactions. They focus on non-transactional aspects of the business and, hence, are much less dependent on IT.

Their expectations mainly focus on timely and accurate information and metrics digital dashboards to provide business insights based on transaction data and patterns. Business analytics is a major tool this group benefits from.

Vice president of sales

Sales is another critical function in any company. The sales team is the face of the company for customers, and its members are responsible for all front-end activities. Their priorities are revenue, forecasting, and sales team efficiency. In most companies, they are also responsible for managing all sales and fulfillment channels, such as sales representatives (reps) or distributors.

Their expectations from IT can be substantial, as they are involved in many day-to-day activities, both inside and outside company. They want tools to improve their efficiency and their ability to forecast and manage revenue. They want good customer engagement systems (customer relationship management—CRM), revenue forecasting, and attainment tools. They also need tools to manage distribution channel partners to understand what's going on with their pass through sales and inventory levels.

Sales teams also benefit heavily from business analytics and metrics dashboards that can deliver actionable intelligence to them. Sales VPs also wants IT to help them ensure that sales teams are spending most of their time on customers and not wasting time pulling together or manipulating data.

VP of R&D / chief technology officer (CTO)

Research and development (R&D) teams for any company are the backbone of the company's future. That's where new products are conceived and brought to fruition to drive the next wave of company growth. R&D priorities are always on innovation and new product time to market. Although they are not involved with day-to-day sales and shipping, they are often under a lot of pressure to deliver the next great thing quickly.

Depending upon the nature of the industry, their expectations for IT can be huge. In the high-tech electronics world of chip design, many times you see independent IT engineering teams, while the core IT team focuses only on infrastructure. I have never seen an IT team involved in direct software development. Most just support the infrastructure required by R&D engineers.

The CTO's expectations from IT are to ensure that all R&D systems and infrastructure are always available. Also, that their scientists are not losing valuable time due to system disruptions. In some industries, R&D experiments/simulations can be very time-consuming and expensive. Losing experimental data could cost the company money and sometimes a missed opportunity.

VP of marketing / chief marketing officer (CMO)

A company marketing team, separate from the product marketing team, prioritizes maintaining the company's external persona. They are also responsible for influencing external stakeholders, from customers to investors and the public at large. Marketing today is much more digital and has grown to depend heavily on information technology. Many Chief Marketing Officers have genuinely unique needs in addition to typical back-office automation. Their priorities are focused on external influence mechanisms.

Many times, their expectations are not met well by traditional IT depart-ments because many don't have the expertise in externally focused digi-tal technologies. Many marketing departments have their own IT teams, whether in-house or external, managing the digital aspects of their function.

VP of manufacturing / product delivery

For any company, this is the most crucial function, ensuring products or services are successfully delivered on time, intact, and accurately. Even in today's world of outsourced manufacturing, this function remains the most critical. In many ways, outsourcing manufacturing actually adds a level of complexity.

Manufacturing's priorities are to ensure that the supply chain is function-ing well. In most industries, the supply chain now has four to six major stages, including suppliers, logistics providers, manufacturers, distribu-tors, retailers, and consumers. By any comparison, this is probably the most complex function in any company, requiring successful implemen-tation on multiple levels. That includes the smooth flow of material in and out of factories, correctly scheduling orders, effective use of equipment, etc., and most importantly, controlling manufacturing costs, including the cost of raw materials.

Given the scope of their function, manufacturing's needs and expecta-tions are huge. They want to make sure all IT systems and infrastructure are running without a hitch and do not have a negative effect on any of the above performance metrics. A secondary expectation is that IT can improve manufacturing/delivery efficiency across all business processes, from purchasing to manufacturing to shipping. This group is genuine-ly focused on continuous improvement in all aspects of manufacturing—efficiency, quality, cost, productivity, and speed. That, in turn, requires a lot of help from IT on a continuous basis.

Although very demanding, manufacturing teams are also very much equal partners in all projects and work very effectively with IT teams. They are always in the trenches with IT teams and have a good appreciation of the value IT associates bring to the table.

VP of supply chain, logistics, and procurement

This is a critical role in most physical-product companies that requires purchasing and moving raw materials or finished products. In companies that do not sell a physical product, this function is mostly generic in nature. This group directly influences the company's bottom line in companies that manufacture a tangible product. Their priorities include ensuring the smooth supply of raw materials from suppliers to plants and then from plants to distribution centers to retailers. Their function involves partnerships with raw material suppliers and shipping providers. In most companies, this function is also responsible for incoming and outgoing warehouse management.

Just like all other departments, supply chain planning departments also have tactical and strategic needs. Their tactical needs include purchasing systems, material planning systems, supply chain planning and scheduling systems, shipping and billing systems, and supplier collaboration systems.

On a strategic level, their IT needs include business analytics and systems to manage their suppliers' performance, costs, and quality. The most complex of their IT needs is the supply chain planning and scheduling system. The more complex the supply chain, the more complex the planning and scheduling associated with it. Unlike ERP systems that capture transactions, planning and scheduling systems are driven by assumptions and, therefore, can never be 100 percent accurate. Supply chain teams all want IT to help them automate the planning process and make it 100 percent accurate all the time, even though a lot of variables and subjective assumptions are involved. I have not seen a successful supply chain planning system for that reason.

Communities

In the above section, we discussed specific company roles, their priorities, and their expectations of IT. In addition to the teams that perform these functions, several vital communities depend heavily on IT. They are also crucial stakeholders and have many expectations. These communities are employees, customers, suppliers, and distributors. It is a little tricky to understand such communities' expectations because direct communication isn't really possible. It's much easier for CIOs to sit with the VP of sales and talk about their priorities and expectations than it is to sit with each employee, customer, supplier, or distributor.

However, it remains the CIO's role to understand the pulse of these communities and live up to their expectations. This aspect is by far the most challenging for any CIO. These are not homogenous communities. Each has many subsets. Different segments of these communities have different opinions based on their individual experiences with IT.

Let's look at some commonalities among these four communities.

Employees
Employees or End Users, as IT often refers to them, are the real consumers of all IT services. Their priorities are to be as productive as they possibly can and focus on their work. However, to do that, they need lots of IT tools. They have both generic and specific needs. Generic needs include tools like laptops, desktops, phones, tablets, network connectivity, productivity software, etc. Their specific needs depend upon what they do in a company and the tools they need to perform those duties.

In general, they expect to have best in class technology. They are usually not aware of the costs of IT solutions. They prefer the latest and greatest hardware and software. They prefer constraints be eliminated or minimized. They like to work as freely as possible. Security is important to them as long as it doesn't interfere with getting the job done. They don't want to be burdened with unnecessary procedures.

However, collectively, they are the most significant community CIOs serve, and a CIO's primary responsibility is to make them as efficient as possible.

Customers

This community may not consume IT services directly, but they do experience the effects of technology. As a customer, their priorities are well defined. They want the best product or service at best possible price and with best experience. They want to have a pleasant experience and do business easily before, during and after they purchase products or services.

In most businesses, they neither see nor interact with IT associates directly, unless they are involved in IT projects required for connecting two businesses. However, customers know whether their experience is seamless or if product quality meets their expectations, which depends primarily on IT systems working behind the scenes.

They also expect businesses to use the latest technology. If your company lags in technology, it will almost certainly have a negative effect on your product or service quality, speed of delivery, ease of doing business, and cost.

If IT departments don't interact with customers directly, how would they assess IT value from the customer's perspective? The most common way is to work with the other departments in the company that do interact with customers directly, such as sales, marketing, shipping, or customer service.

One inherent weakness in solely relying on secondary feedback from other departments about end customer perspectives is that you may or may not get the real facts. All that feedback will come flavored with the opinion of whoever passes on the feedback.

Depending upon the nature of your business, the definition of a customer may be broad enough to include distributors who act as an intermediary between your company and the consumer. However, distributors are independent businesses that write you checks for the products they buy from you to resell. In that context, I would recommend putting distributors and their expectations in the same category as customers. However, understanding the value of IT and what's working by interacting with distributors is much easier than interacting with customers directly.

Suppliers

Another community that heavily depends on IT services is suppliers. The term suppliers here includes all material and services vendors.

With this community, you are a customer, but they still depend on your IT technology and have expectations of IT. IT teams may or may not directly interact with suppliers, but like the customer community, suppliers also feel the effects of good or bad IT technology.

Supplier priorities are simple. They want to sell you as much as they can at the highest acceptable price and ensure that you are 100 percent satisfied with their services so you will come back for more products and services. Suppliers also want long-term relationships, which invests them in your success.

Their expectations from your company are for you to be easy to do business with, that you have high-quality forecast information that can help them meet your needs, and that you pay them accurately and on time.

All these expectations need sound IT technology behind the scenes—technology that may include a good forecasting system, a material requirements planning (MRP) system, procurement systems, supplier portal, business-to-business (B2B) transactions systems to enable the massive volume of transactions, material visibility system, quality and inspection systems, and so on.

If your company is not powered by all the necessary technologies behind the scenes, the supplier will feel the effects and have a poor value perception of your IT department. If that perception is translating into poor business results, IT has a stake in improving the value proposition.

CIOs who are purely technical or introverts shy away from trying to understand the pulse of all these communities and their perception of

IT. That creates a misalignment between IT and these communities over time and leads to an unsustainable situation. CIOs must develop extrovert skills to engage with such communities and proactively understand their perceptions.

If you are a CIO, you might say that many of these expectations are unreasonable. However, most users/stakeholders would beg to differ. They think these expectations are very reasonable because understanding these communities is a vital part of business operations.

From the IT side, we have the luxury of seeing the diverse spectrum and variations in expectations and needs. That naturally puts IT leaders in the position of finding solutions that work for as many IT customers as possible and prioritizing those customers based on the company's strategic goals. Unfortunately, that sometimes means prioritizing an end user over the CEO. That's the crux of IT-business alignment—figuring out which priorities are most important and how IT should respond.

CHAPTER 6

Value Delivery Mechanism: IT-Business Alignment

It's not that complicated

We have discussed aspects of IT's business value, how it's measured, who measures it, and what they look for. Now, the most important discussion centers on the real mechanism CIOs use to understand, define, and deliver business value—IT-Business Alignment.

Stories abound about the lack of IT-business alignment which leads to the perceived ineffectiveness of IT. Just like value discussions, I have participated in many CIO conversations about what is IT-Business alignment, how to ensure one, what works for them, and what doesn't? It's noteworthy that these discussions are occurring among CIOs because this is something many IT departments struggle with. Alignment is an evergreen topic in most CIO conferences. If IT-Business alignment were easy and crisply defined, there wouldn't be much discussion about it. Nor would there be any success or failure stories to be studied.

The following is a five-step approach that has worked well for me. When I am have just become CIO at a new company, I spend much of my time in the first few months to understand the situation using this framework. I then use what I have learned to build an IT strategy. This task must be done quickly because you will be expected to present a high-level, strategic plan within the first ninety days. The steps include:

1. Understand your company's business and its ecosystem.
2. Understand your company's mission in that ecosystem.
3. Understand the company's personality.
4. Identify the business drivers that keep the company humming.
5. Develop mechanisms to ensure IT support for all levels of the organization.

From conversations I've had about IT-business alignment, I see most focus only on the last step in the list above. That step is necessary, but by itself, it is unlikely to provide sound IT-business alignment. In fact, this step alone is meaningless if you disregard the first four building blocks.

As you will see at the end of this discussion, the profile developed by using this framework is unique to each company. While there are many commonalities, all companies are unique, so what works in one may fail mightily in another. I can tell from personal experience that the role of CIO is never the same from company to company. Even for companies within the same industry, IT strategies based on these five steps are always unique to that company. In all practical matters, each new company is different, with different missions, different risk profiles, different personalities, different tolerance levels, and different expectations. You can't use one IT strategy when companies differ so drastically.

The point is: You will need to create a unique plan after studying the first four elements above. Let's look at developing this unique profile that you can then use to develop a long-lasting IT-business alignment.

1. Understand your company's business and its ecosystem.

This step is crucial. You must start from here, with a very high-level picture from the outside looking in. In broader terms, understanding the ecosystem means understanding everything there is to know about the company. This is a very fundamental step, but many folks fail to give it enough importance upfront, which inevitably leads to a misalignment between what you do in IT and what's expected of you. I am surprised by how many folks who have been working at the same company for many years do not have a good understanding of their company's external ecosystem.

You want to understand your company's surroundings as well as its unique characteristics. The best way to develop a picture of a company's ecosystem is by answering dozens of questions in multiple categories. The following list is not exhaustive but should give you an excellent idea of what kind of information is necessary for building this unique company profile.

Products—What exactly does the company sell? What are its products and/or services? Are products/services tangible or difficult to comprehend? What exactly is the value these products deliver to clients?

Customers—Whom do you sell to? What do those customers do with these products or services? For example, how do they consume, and what exactly do they get from the product/service? Do they buy raw material to build their product or do they consume your finished product themselves? Is this a B2B sale (business to business selling) or B2C (business to consumer selling). If your customers are not the ultimate consumers, who are their customers?

Competitors—Who are the major players in the industry? Who are the company's key competitors, directly competing with your products and/ or services? How are they different from your company? What are their financial strengths and weaknesses?

This factor is important because there is a good chance you will be answering one question, probably over a hundred times in a year—"How do our competitors do this?" Whether you are talking about strategy, cost, a project, or risk management, people have some fascination with comparing themselves to their competitors. You, as a CIO, are expected to know the answer. If your company is not the industry leader, then expect the questions about competitors to be asked about pretty much everything you do as CIO.

Sales channels—How do they sell: online, in retail stores, through distribution channels, through sales channels? Different channels bring different dynamics and challenges.

Industry—What macro industry does your company play in? How big is the industry? What is the total available market (TAM) as reported by leading market research firms tracking your industry? Which independent research firms monitor the progress of your industry? What leading industry associations or consortiums monitor the industry's dynamics? What are the short- and long-term trends? Is this industry growing or shrinking? What are the threats to this industry? Are there substantial technical or financial barriers to entry? What disruptions are likely over the next five to ten years? Who are the leaders and followers? Where does your company stand? Is it a leader fighting to maintain the leadership position, or is it a small player growing to become relevant and looking to become the new leader in the next ten years? Is this a highly regulated or mostly entrepreneurial new industry? Does it have a lot of inherent compliance and regulatory risks?

How old and mature is this industry? The older the industry, the more rigid it is. The newer an industry, the more modern and creative its norms will be. How mature is the industry from a digitization and automation perspective? How efficient is the supply chain?

Stage in the supply chain—Where does your company fit in the overall supply chain from raw materials, manufacturer of subassembly (component), manufacturer of the product, distributor, logistics provider, retailers, to consumer.

Understanding your position in the whole value chain is vital to understanding the dynamics your company is subjected to. Companies closer to the consumer have different burdens than companies on the far-left end of the supply chain, closest to the raw material. Also, the level of competition depends mostly upon which end of the value chain you play in.

Often these supply chains are complicated. In some cases, you may not know more than one supply chain node on either side of where your company sits.

Investors, shareholders, owners—Who are the company's investors, shareholders, and/or owners? Is this a publicly traded company, or is it privately owned by a family or group of private equity investors? How broad is the investor base? What percentage of the company is owned by external investors versus insiders? Are there any institutional investors or just family and friends? Is this considered a growth or value stock?

The nature of company ownership dictates the structure of the board of directors, which in turn dictates the governance and priorities of management. Have investors been rewarded well for owning these shares, either through equity gain or dividends over time? Are investors in for the long haul or just making a quick buck?

Company financials—What do your company's financials look like? If it's a publicly traded corporation, there will be a lot of public information available. There is a wealth of data on historical trends, current snapshots, and future prospects.

Take the time to understand all the key financial statements (income, cash flow, and balance sheet), recognize the historical patterns of each statement over the last few years, understand gross margins and operating margins, and understand the debt situation and whether the company is showing a constant rise in shareholder equity or dwindling. Does the company have healthy operating margins and positive cash flow every quarter, or is it struggling to make ends meet?

Go through the company's latest 10Q and 10K reports filed with the Securities and Exchange Commission (SEC) which discuss all business details, future potential, risks, etc. Also, find out if there are any publicly identified risks—any public comments, lawsuits, or competition lawsuits.

The best place to start learning about the company's ecosystem is searching its stock ticker (for publicly traded companies) and reviewing financials, ratios, financial reports, analyst reports, and listening to the last quarter's earnings call from company executives. There is no better place to get the pulse of the company and its ecosystem than merely browsing the available public information.

Just imagine a picture of any company before and after answering all these questions. Once you have this information, your entire view of the company is much different. It's a lot more educated and informed. That knowledge is critical in developing a proper IT strategy.

2. Understand your company's mission in that ecosystem.

Knowing the company's ecosystem and environment from outside is one thing, but you also need to know the company from the inside out. The two basic tasks in this step are: 1) Understand the value proposition your company provides or how it differentiates itself from others in the industry; 2) Understand the exact mission of your company in navigating the industry they are in.

Understanding these things is critical for any CIO because the company's mission drives its short-term priorities, which, in turn, drives the CIO's priorities. Your primary goal as CIO is to ensure that you are working on priorities that support the company's mission while ensuring that other non-value-added priorities don't become hurdles. Knowing the mission will allow you to determine what's essential and what's not.

IT roadmaps are different for different companies based on each company's mission. For example, for a startup company focusing on their first product, the only mission could be the successful launch of that first product. That could be a make or break event for the company. Another company may be fighting legal or regulatory battles and may be focused on nothing but getting out of that bad situation. Yet another company may have been in business for over fifty years but is fighting new, disruptive trends or new competitors and is solely focused on revamping its innovation process to remain relevant into the next business cycle.

As companies mature from startup to established to small, then medium, and then large-scale enterprises, their needs change. What was acceptable when a company was small could be a significant issue when it grows to be a large enterprise spread around the world with tens of thousands of employees. As companies grow, their risk tolerance also changes, which, in turn, changes the priorities and expectations of technology.

Please know the difference between the real mission the CEO is driving versus the generic and abstract mission statement you may find on the website, in company presentations, and in company literature. The real mission the CEO is driving is what really matters.

In the past, I have developed three-year roadmaps based on each company's mission. In each case, my three-year roadmaps were entirely different. In one case, it was all about scaling up the systems so we could support a tenfold increase in volume and revenue over the next few years. In another case, it was all about expanding the use of technology in all corners of the company, across all layers to improve productivity, efficiency, and quality through consistency.

The bottom line is no one can begin to conceptualize IT priorities without adequately understanding what the CEO's mission is for that company for the next three to five years. If you try to develop a roadmap without adequately understanding the mission, it's guaranteed to fail. It may not even get the necessary attention for initial presentation as you socialize that roadmap. If CIOs develop roadmaps based only on the IT point of view or driven only by technology or IT infrastructure, it won't even come close to relating to the company's mission. Misalignment begins right there.

IT is a generic solution that must be custom-fitted to each company's needs. Without that custom fit, all you have is a lot of technology without focus or purpose.

3. Understand the company's personality.

As we discussed in the previous chapter, subjective value is more important than objective value as defined by metrics alone. We also discussed
ways to understand subjective value as seen from the perspective of various stakeholders. However, none of that explains a company's personality.
It's the company's unique character that explains how it operates. People
sometimes refer to this as company culture, which is intangible but real. It
explains how companies respond to situations.

An organization's culture or personality is defined by how it operates day
to day as well as strategically. CIOs need to understand that culture excep-
tionally well because any given approach may be rewarded in one company while the same action is punished in another. However, understand
that one culture isn't necessarily better than another. Different cultures
make perfect sense at different companies, and they all can produce very
creditable results. However, understanding a company's personality is
crucial from the CIO's strategic alignment perspective.

No definitive method exists for understanding a company's culture, but
you can get a good idea based on how a company behaves in various situations. The list of characteristics below gives you a good idea of a company's personality.

- Does it tolerate and encourage risk-taking or punish people
  for taking chances?
- Does it make decisions top down or bottoms up? Are decisions made by the few on top, or is it a consensus-driven bot-
  tom-up decision-making environment?
- Do leaders have the right technical depth in their areas as op-
  posed to being a generic leader?
- Do leaders make tough but logical calls, and are they able to
  convince others to come along?
- Do leaders make timely decisions with or without perfect
  information, or do they go into analysis paralysis mode for
  everything?

- Do leaders take responsibility for their decisions, and are they held accountable? Or is the blame game the norm?
- Does the company reward collaboration and communication?
- Does it rely on technical analysis in decision making or the gut feelings of a few?
- Does it have non-negotiable principles and what are they?
- Do teams follow top-down directives well or only sometimes?
- Does it have the highest regard for business ethics and statutory compliance?
- Does it have the highest regard for the law of the land and a zero-tolerance policy for any illegal acts? Even simple acts like unauthorized use of software give you a good sense of what a company tolerates and what it doesn't.
- Does it have a clear strategic vision, or does it operate mostly tactically from quarter to quarter?
- Does it highly value customers, employees, and suppliers and insist on 100 percent integrity in business operations?
- Does it spend lavishly or skimp on necessary spending? This is especially important because, based on spending inclination, CIOs can figure out which level of IT service—bronze, silver, gold or platinum—is appropriate for that company.
- Does it have a highly centralized or decentralized decision-making and execution process?
- Does it use a metric-driven approach or more of a qualitative, ad-hoc, decision-based process?

This list gives you an idea of what defines a company's culture. You can also see why understanding this is important for CIOs trying to build the necessary IT-business alignment.

The above list sheds light on general characteristics, but there are other subtleties that you must know, such as who the most influential and least influential leaders are. You would be surprised how, in the end, decisions are made by the influential few. They get their influence not necessarily from their area of responsibility, but more from their attitude, maturity, honesty, and integrity, among other things. It's not very difficult to see who is highly respected in the company and who is not. The highly respected people have a way of influencing many decisions well beyond their area of responsibility. I have seen many CIOs who could influence many areas outside of IT. I have also seen well-respected CFOs, manufacturing, operations, sales executives, and legal counsels who exert influence well beyond their function. This influence is more driven by who they are as a person than their position in the company.

CIOs need to understand such influence centers. I always go to an influential personality to run ideas by them and get an early indication of how those ideas are likely to be received once announced. If you can get influential people on board with your ideas, you can count on them for support when you experience resistance from other corners. The opposite holds true in that even if you get positive support from other stakeholders, influential personalities can keep you from getting very far with an idea.

4. Identify the business drivers that keep the company humming.

Knowing who holds sway is good, but one also needs to understand the key business drivers that keep the company humming. In every company, some functions are considered mainstream and their effective operation is essential. Even a small hiccup in those functions can have negative consequences. Then there are many sideline functions that are essential but not necessarily mainstream. They are overhead or support functions. The hiccups in those functions may not have significant, negative consequences but should be monitored.

For example, manufacturing or service delivery is considered mission-critical. The same is true for sales or product management—their work drives direct revenue, while legal, HR, IT, or marketing needs do not. Mainstream drivers are more important to the company's success than other functions.

This aspect is crucial. Many IT best practices insist on steering committees and a consensus-driven project portfolio. However, my experience has been that such policy- and process-heavy organizations don't implement the tough and deliberate prioritization necessary for accomplishing the company's success. Such a model makes decisions by steering committee, relying on votes and consensus, where support function priorities become equal to sales or manufacturing priorities, irrespective of the direct effect on the top and bottom lines. That kind of consensus-driven approach invariably takes focus away from critical priorities, while much time is spent on priorities with little value from the CEO's perspective.

Remember, IT project decisions are investment decisions. Such investments should be driven by the potential for positive outcomes and not based on a democratic process. A company's real success or failure depends upon making the right bets and not losing time with less value-added activities. If you are not able to make a distinction between the two kinds of investments, you will end up losing focus on critical priorities.

One may wonder, if you have a strong IT steering committee, then why is there any misalignment? It's because of the way those committees are structured and how priorities are judged. Many times, leaders in key areas, such as manufacturing, R&D, or sales, may not even show up to steering committee meetings because they perceive them as political discussions that offer no potential upside. In such cases, these leaders figure out alternative ways to get their needs addressed, either with or without IT support. That's how misalignment begins.

The crux of the story is IT-business alignment is a relationship management matter and not a process or policy matter. Alignment happens between people, not departments. CIOs need to know which departments are delivering direct value and which are delivering indirect value.

5. Develop mechanisms to ensure IT support for all levels of the organization.

Once you understand the industry, the company, and its mission and culture, you will have an excellent idea for what to focus on. You also get a good idea about who your best allies are and how to be effective in your environment. Then you need to take that last step and formalize the IT-business alignment.

The critical foundation of this alignment is understanding alignment happens between people and not between departments. That means communication and collaboration between all members of IT and other departments at all levels is critical. It also means all sides are kept apprised of what is happening so they can figure out how to help. It also requires defined communication guidelines.

Alignment can't just be between a CIO and their peers at the executive leadership level. The alignment needs to reach all levels to allow IT to focus on all aspects of the partnership. Let's illustrate this by an example. The CIO and the general manager can align on whether a specific investment is right for the business and worth focusing their collective energies on. Then second level directors from both sides can focus on aligning resources to make that happen. They can partner on the best solution, the timeframe, required resources, adoption mechanisms, roles and responsibilities, etc. Then the third level of alignment would occur between project managers and key users. They would focus on the granular details within the project plan, testing, design approvals, etc. Finally, the fourth level of alignment occurs between two associates—IT and department associates assigned to work on specific tasks.

The above is an example, but this multi-level alignment is crucial in almost every aspect of IT work, be it related to projects or even routine tasks like updating software or emergency notifications. Having this multi-level approach is key to ensuring we have alignment between IT and all departments, and it facilitates sorting out issues appropriately.

Another important aspect of IT-business alignment is scheduled, formal, bidirectional communication, which helps get everyone on the same page. That means having a defined meeting schedule, usually on a quarterly or monthly basis, to review priorities, project progress, resolve issues, and provide help as needed.

We also use standard communication templates for discussing project investments, progress, and financials. The more defined the communication, the more effective the alignment.

Using this alignment and formal communication structure cuts the surprise factor to negligible levels, which, in turn, ensures tight alignment. Most misalignment problems seem to occur when IT teams work in isolation with little or no contact with end users. That's a recipe for failure because IT is not a technical department; IT is a customer service department where technology is the service.

CHAPTER 7

Step Up the Value Curve

IT can be divided into three categories based on capabilities and effectiveness. All IT departments go through a maturity curve that enhances their effectiveness and contributions to business operations over time. The value curve below depicts the three distinct stages of IT maturity.

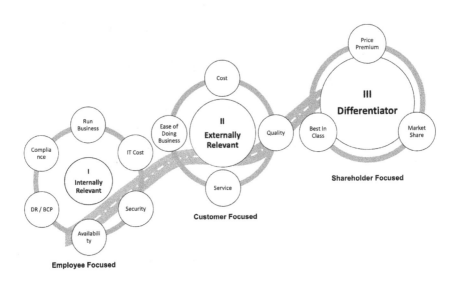

Figure 7-1: The Value Curve

Level I: Internally Relevant: Most IT departments fall into this category. Such IT departments serve an essential mission of managing critical IT operations focused on serving users' needs. Such IT departments are mostly internally focused and serve all the most basic essential elements expected from an IT department. They also ensure all the systems, network, and hardware are running round the clock so no business operation is negatively impacted while also balancing IT costs and risks.

IT departments at Level I on the value curve are critical for running the business operation in all aspects. Any deficiencies in IT operations almost always leads to negative consequences for any company. However, Level I type IT departments are far removed from the company's end customer.

Level II: Externally Relevant: This type of IT department is more mature in its capabilities and contributions to the company's bottom line. The value of such IT departments is much higher than that of a Level I departments. Level II departments focus on the company's end customer and are involved in all aspects of customer engagement processes. They are intensely involved in both front office and back office operations. In these types of IT organizations, you will find many IT associates have a comprehensive understanding of the company's customers and products, and the nitty-gritty details of what matters to end customers. Usually, these types of IT departments spend much effort in enhancing customers' ease of doing business and those things that matter to customers, such as cost, service, quality, etc.

Level II IT departments on the value curve are truly externally relevant in addition to their primary mission of performing internally relevant functions. These IT departments are critical not only in the eyes of employees, but more importantly, in the eyes of the customers who pay the bills for everyone in the company.

Level III: Technology as Key Differentiator: This type of IT department is one step ahead because it is not only relevant internally and externally, but it is also at the center of the company's core competency. Such IT departments are often involved in projects that change the company's standing in the industry and among its competitors. These IT departments focus on shareholders, in addition to focusing on employees and customers. Such IT departments are truly a strategic component of a company and focus on the shareholders' long-term interests. They are involved in projects that help their company gain market share by developing state-of-the-art products or developing the capabilities that stand out from the rest of the competitors. This is the maturity stage on the value curve where IT capabilities are truly differentiating factors for the company. Such IT capabilities will be why customers will choose the company over its competitors.

Amazon's IT capabilities on its e-commerce platform is the best example of Level III—the differentiating type of IT. That's when your IT capabilities help your company stand out from the competition. Many more examples exist of such companies where information technology differentiates the company's standing in the marketplace, such as Uber, Airbnb, Apple, and Google.

What drives an IT department's level of maturity? The first element is the CIO's capabilities, along with other C-suite executives' deep understanding of the real potential of Information Technologies for their mission. CEOs don't need to be IT experts, but if they understand the potential of information technology in their mission, they will drive different level of expectations from their IT departments. Those expectations, in turn, drive what type of CIO one needs and the required skills of all the IT associates underneath.

In my assessment, well over two-thirds of IT departments fall somewhere between Level I and Level II on the value curve. Some make it to Level II entirely, but very few make it to Level III.

CIOs can use this high-level journey roadmap to motivate their teams and paint the long-term vision of where they are today and where they could go. This helps associates put in perspective their current work and the journey ahead for the long-term vision of truly becoming a premier IT organization.

CHAPTER 8

Essential Factors for Delivering Value

Because adding tangible business value is vital for IT's success, we discussed what value is and isn't, who measures the value, and how it is measured. We also talked about key stakeholders, their expectations, and their subjective assessments of value. We discussed the big picture of how to deliver that value through an IT-business-alignment mechanism. Now let's look at essential factors for delivering the business value.

Four key things set success apart from failure when delivering business value:

1. The mindset: Never forget that you are the business.
2. Embedding IT in the field: IT is a service function.
3. Business pull, not technology push.
4. Lead the way: Prudent IT cost-management is the least you can do.

Let's now look at each of these items in more detail.

The mindset: Never forget you are the business.

When you talk to any member of an IT team, you will hear them using expressions that include the word "business." For example, "Business wants to use that tool," "Business isn't ready," "Business made that decision," or "Our business doesn't really understand IT." It took me a while to understand exactly what was meant by "business." While the whole world refers to a company as a business, you would not expect any one person or department within a company referred to as a business. I thought people were using the term to refer to the company itself, which would make perfect sense. However, then I realized they were referring to the users of the functions/departments they serve, like sales, finance, manufacturing, and operations as a business. In other words, a group of people in all these functions are referred to as business, and everyone in IT is referred to as IT.

Only IT folks refer to everyone and everything else as business. Even when you have a large cross-functional team, you will see that IT folks are referring to themselves as IT and everyone else as business. However, I have never heard anyone from any of those other departments refer to themselves or others as business. They refer to themselves by the name of the function they are representing.

This expression, which defines us as IT and everyone else as business, is the most significant self-inflicted wound IT teams carry, without even knowing the considerable damage it causes to their success.

The expression has two major mindset flaws. The first is that it divides the company into us (IT) versus them (Business), which makes it difficult to work as one team. Then every aspect of a project, task, or any responsibility is divided into us (IT) and them (Business). The whole mindset of dealing with all users becomes a two-party partnership instead of a one-team approach of dealing with everything together. This mindset divides the roles, tasks, responsibilities, money, and even accountability. It is also the primary cause of either party blaming the other because such a two-party mechanism is enabled in every aspect of IT work. If all the team members work as one team, they can collectively succeed or fail together as one team so the question of one party versus the other doesn't come up. Working as a team also affects who gets the credit for the work done versus who gets the blame for whatever small portion didn't work. With two parties, both like to take credit, and both like to blame. Once again, this two-party structure systematically enables this divide.

Secondly, and most importantly, this mindset excludes IT from being an integral part of the company. This phenomenon pretty much broadcasts to the world that IT folks are not part of the business. As a CIO, you must understand you are the business first and IT second. You must change the mindset of all IT team members so they will not consider themselves of any less value than anyone else in the company. If every other associate in the company is referred to as "business" for doing their work, IT associates should equally be referred as "business" for doing their IT work.

The negative consequences of this phenomenon go well beyond just the labels. This mindset negatively impacts IT teams' ability to become an integral part of the whole company. It also prevents them from looking at a problem from the company or user's perspective because their mindset is IT and the other party is business. It, unfortunately, precipitates their thought that they don't need to understand any aspect of the business. The business users will do the job of understanding what a problem means to the company while IT folks can focus on the technology side of the problem. You can see how this exclusion drives the whole involvement of IT folks away from understanding the full picture. That is, however, essential for enabling technical solutions that are in the company's best interests. Such exclusion greatly prevents them from learning exact business processes and why they are necessary for the company's success.

I will candidly admit that even though I have been noticing this mindset and its expressions for the last twenty years, I have not been able to change it completely in my teams. Despite educating IT folks about the negative consequences of this mindset, I still hear them say the same thing. Worse, I see CIOs and industry executive coaches also refer to this two-party IT and business system.

This whole issue of IT-Business alignment that we discussed in the last chapter stems from this very mindset of us as IT and everyone else as business. The reason we must work so hard on establishing and nurturing that alignment is because this mindset has already created a divide in our approach to solving every problem.

You must understand that you are not IT only. You are business first and IT second. Without knowing that business process or without IT as an integral part of the business, there is no business. Don't leave yourself out and then wonder why you are not getting a proper IT-business alignment. Think and act like you are a business, and then see the magic of how well you can help all those functions to help your business (company) thrive.

Embed IT in the field—IT is a service function.

IT delivers the best results when it's embedded in all departments. Most CIOs in large companies now have staff called "Business Liaisons." In this role, a team member is responsible for all IT activities for a specific department (finance, sales, R&D, etc.). Their job is to understand the IT needs of the department they are assigned to. In effect, in sales terminology, they are internal account managers. They are sometimes even dotted-line reporting to those respective department heads and they participate in major departmental meetings to stay apprised of activities in that department.

If possible, this person should physically sit inside those departments instead of sitting in the IT area. Depending upon the size of the company and/or department, there could even be a whole team focusing on a particular department's processes. If that's the case, those IT teams are better off physically sitting alongside users, instead of the relative isolation of sitting with the rest of the IT team.

Embedding IT personnel in departments works like magic for both users and IT. Not much is lost in translation, nor is there extra work in communicating priorities. Remember, IT is a customer service function first. If you look at any IT project, over 70 percent of the effort relates to non-technical activities.

The typical IT project life cycle involves problem definition, solution formulation, development or configuration, testing, training, and deployment. If you look at this whole cycle, every stage except development is teamwork and depends largely upon the consumers of that particular solution. All that work requires non-technical skills—communication, alignment, understanding purpose and priorities, understanding individual personalities etc. In other words, all those stages require strong, interpersonal collaboration and aren't really about the technology. There is no better way to accomplish this strong connection than putting IT and user teams together for the project's duration, or indefinitely in the case of large departments that stress CI (continuous improvement).

It is also the reason it is difficult for IT staff to work remotely. Despite all the new remote collaboration technologies, nothing can match the success of teams working together as one with lots of face to face communication.

Business pull, not technology push.

The third essential factor for delivering value is your approach. Is your roadmap created with a business pull or a technology push approach? These are two distinctly different approaches, even though they may seem similar.

I have always argued that business pull priorities are the only ones CIOs should work on beyond backend technology infrastructure. A business pull approach ensures you are working on your company's and all departments' priorities instead of pushing your independent vision driven by the latest and greatest technology.

Many IT departments still run in technology push mode and don't even realize it. This happens when you have CIOs who come predominantly from a technology background and are more comfortable with technology than people or business process. They understand the technology well, but unfortunately, they are not as connected with the company's mission and vision.

The pure technological background of CIOs also affects their ability to pull c-suite peers into understanding IT and its potential. If benefactors of IT solutions don't understand technology and CIOs aren't capable of bridging the divide, then users don't know what to seek from IT.

It's very easy to see if IT roadmap is based on a technology push or business pull. If the roadmap is created with project priorities that directly translate to key performance indicators (KPIs) such as revenue, market share, cost of goods sold (COGS), margin improvement, productivity, quality, etc., then it is a business pull roadmap.

On the contrary, if an IT roadmap shows projects in technical terms such as system upgrade, storage upgrade, Cloud adoption, operating system upgrade, data center consolidation, virtualization, backup, etc., then it's predominantly a technology push approach.

In the business pull approach, you start with expectations of a particular result that is tied to business KPIs and then figure out what IT solutions are required to meet those objectives. In the tech-push approach, IT teams start with the newest fade in the market, and they are convinced it adds significant value to business KPIs, however remote the connection may be.

CIOs who are using technology-push approaches aren't bad. They are working with the best intentions trying to deliver an effective solution that supports business KPIs. However, as we find in every project, the only projects that deliver real, lasting value are the ones that fill a need and are embraced by users from start to finish. Technology-push projects are created by IT leaders trying to demonstrate how the result will enhance business KPIs. Sometimes these projects succeed and sometimes they don't.

However, CIOs cannot depend solely on delivering whatever is requested by other departments. You must put forward the best technology solutions. In some cases, CIOs even have to take the lead in identifying the problem and the solution as well.

Another aspect of business pull versus technology push is the art of making business-driven technology decisions and not technology-driven business decisions. Let's look at what this means.

Business-driven technology decisions are the ones that start with identifying some business problem and then identifying the technology solution for solving that problem. For example, your sales VP is looking to improve revenue, sales attainment, and efficiency. You may naturally explore some CRM solutions that address that need. Moreover, in this process, you may start with what exactly is needed to solve those problems and then look for CRM systems that can address those needs. That's a business-driven technology decision to pick a technology that solves the problem.

In many cases, I see the exact opposite—CIOs or sales VPs start implementing the latest and greatest CRM system (read: most hyped or flavor of the month) based on marketing and anecdotal evidence. They start adopting systems, usually figuring out that a given CRM system is used by their competitors, so they implement it themselves. With this approach, you rarely see a solution that matches the business problem you are trying to solve, let alone focusing on business KPIs or making a real business case for implementing the new solution. It becomes a CRM implementation project instead of sales improvement project.

In this latter case, you have already made a technology decision and are expecting certain business results that may or may not come.

Another drawback with a technology-driven business decision is how it may change business processes. In many cases, if you start with the tool and its capabilities/limitations and then define your business process around it, it may not be compatible with your culture, industry, or business conduct. In that event, you are stuck with changing your company for the sake of technology.

While business pull projects are more successful, there are instances when technology push projects can be effective if you don't have a well-defined business process to begin with. Then the technology solution drives standard business processes and disciplines that were not already in place.

With any tech solution, whether business- or tech-driven, you have to be careful not to sacrifice too much of the business process or user buy-in for the sake of staying within the technology's limitations. In the end, any technology is useless unless it's used by someone to deliver value. Otherwise, it's just an expensive asset sitting around accumulating dust.

Lead the way—prudent IT cost management is the least you can do.

In the context of delivering business value by working with your partners and helping them improve KPIs, you can't forget your direct contributions and effect on those KPIs.

The least you can do is ensure you are managing IT costs under your control prudently. Depending upon the size, complexity, and scope of IT services, CIOs are directly responsible for budgets anywhere between 1 to 5 percent of total revenue. That equates to millions and even hundreds of millions of dollars, depending upon the company's size.

No one else understands IT costs better than CIOs. Managing that total cost prudently is the most basic duty of any CIO. It's not very difficult to squander a lot of money in IT. It is also not necessarily true that spending more money ensures success. Nor does it guarantee the success of any particular solution.

Contrary to belief, more IT spending does not necessarily mean better IT or better business results. Understand that IT dollars come straight from profit dollars. In other words, if you reduce IT cost by a dollar, your profit before taxes goes up by a dollar. In this case, a penny saved is indeed a penny earned—in the profit bucket.

If you are managing a hundred-million-dollar annual budget and can save even 5 percent on an annual basis, then your $5 million savings is equivalent to $5 million in profit. So, if your company's profit before tax (PBT) is approximately 10 percent, then that savings is equal to the $50 million in revenue required to generate that profit. If the reductions you make are structural in nature and will recur every year, then you will create $50 million in equivalent value every year without taking any further action.

Given the importance of wise money management in IT budgets, we will focus on how to reduce IT costs without compromising IT services in the Cost Equation section, which is devoted to this subject. We will get into the nitty-gritty details of managing IT costs wisely in several chapters in that section.

In this chapter, we discussed essential factors for delivering business value. These factors, coupled with all the discussion in preceding chapters, helps one put this whole value equation in the right perspective. Recognize that delivering and continuously improving the business value constitutes 70 percent of the CIO's role. If CIOs don't get the value equation right, the other two areas we will discuss won't matter. Every CIO's primary focus must be on business value first and then transition to risk management. Then, at the end, comes the cost management. Between these three factors, cost management is of lesser importance. So let's now focus on the risk management aspect of the CIO's role.

Part III

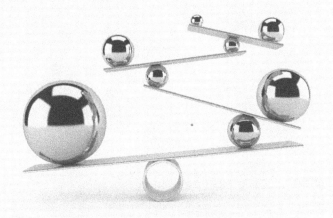

The Risk Equation

Part III

CHAPTER 9

What Does Risk Management Mean to a CIO?

As we discussed earlier, some stakeholders focus on IT strictly from a risk management perspective. For example, the audit committee of the board is tasked with understanding business risks and ensuring proper mitigation is in place. Internal and external auditors of the company or insurance providers would focus exclusively on the risk management aspects of IT. Of course, every CEO and CFO would like to ensure that IT is delivering business value while also managing well the risks under its control.

For CIOs, understanding and managing risks is as important as delivering business value. In the current state, IT probably faces the highest level of risk of all departments in any organization. Information technology is needed not only for the company's success or failure, but it's required as a necessary ingredient in performing every task. In some ways, IT is like the fuel in your car. You can't do much with a car without fuel.

IT risks, if not appropriately managed, can lead to problems that literally stop the company, especially if users are not able to log on to their computers or the company cannot ship products out the door. No other department in any company has this level of risk. Even physical damage to buildings or damage from natural disasters can affect only a portion of the whole company and, therefore, has less impact on the company's overall performance. Of course, no risks are more significant than threats to human life, but here we are discussing risks in the context of running the business operation smoothly.

Risk management is a factor that is always hanging behind the scenes until a tangible incident occurs. As CIO, you are usually laser-focused on business-value-driven projects that improve revenue, profits, and efficiency, and can sometimes get blindsided by other risks. Risks can creep up and do unforgivable damage if not managed actively. IT risks are real, and incidents occur a lot more often than one might think. Once a particular incident occurs, it negatively effects business performance, and focus moves to risk management, albeit in crisis management mode.

Depending upon the current situation, a CIO may be focused 100 percent on risk management and not on business value, especially if a company has just recently experienced a major disaster.

For example, if a company has recently experienced a significant incident such as a massive cyber breach, then the CIO's focus for the next few years will mostly likely be managing cyber risks. Similarly, if a company's data center was affected by a natural disaster and proper disaster recovery infrastructure was not in place, then focus would be on avoiding such risks in the future. The same is true for compliance risks. If a company failed to comply with regulations, it puts the very existence of that company at risk.

IT risk management is unique in the sense that only those with an IT background are qualified to understand and manage those risks. They may also have different risk tolerances than CEOs, CFOs, or audit committee members. In many cases, c-suite executives assume that the majority of IT risks are under control. They presume that understanding and mitigating IT risks proactively is an integral part of being a CIO. If, as a CIO, you don't actively manage those risks, then you are putting your company at risk.

In some cases, the CIO has to explicitly certify adherence to process controls before the CEO or CFO can certify the company is in compliance with given regulations. In that case, you are explicitly taking responsibility for complying with these requirements.

You may not be asked for an update on risk-mitigation projects because others can't relate to the risks. However, you, as a CIO, can't ignore the risks because when incidents occur, nothing else matters. All the good work your IT team has done to enable the company's success can be quickly forgotten because of one adverse event.

Many books have been written about various IT risks and risk mitigation strategies. We will not get into the more in-depth details, but it is worth highlighting some key risks and risk mitigation strategies at a high level. We will do this in the next chapter.

CHAPTER 10

Major Risks Under CIO Ownership

CIOs are accountable for and must manage effectively four major risk categories:

- Operational risks
- Compliance risks
- Disaster recovery and business continuity risks
- Cybersecurity risks

Each of these categories covers a vast array of risks that can be detrimental to the company, and in some extreme cases, put a company out of business. Let's take a little more in-depth look at each of these risk categories and common mitigation strategies that every IT shop should pursue.

Operational risks

These are the most common risks that affect IT services' availability and reliability. Users can tolerate most other service interruptions but not IT service interruptions. Without some IT services, they can't perform their primary duties. If users are not able to access certain software, they are unable to complete their tasks. If users are not able to log in to the email system, they can't communicate or collaborate. If they can't log on to their computers, they pretty much can't do anything.

IT services are not confined to users only. For example, an IT disruption can shut down a company's website, e-commerce site, manufacturing plant, shipping system, order entry system, reservation system, scheduling system, planning and execution system, or customer engagement systems. All such services are considered mission-critical, meaning an outage of even a few minutes could have a tangible, negative effect.

IT operations teams can streamline such service expectations by clearly defining service level agreements (SLAs). SLAs refer to agreements between IT and users about what is acceptable service availability (uptime), response time, or resolution time. This mechanism of defining SLAs acknowledges that it's impossible to ensure 100 percent availability for all services indefinitely.

However, just defining SLAs doesn't mean the risks go away. Depending upon how tight such SLAs are, the CIO may have to invest a lot more money mitigating the risks that threaten your ability to meet the objectives.

Since most IT services depend upon smooth functioning and interplay among hundreds of IT infrastructure components behind the scene, a failure of any one component can render the end service inaccessible. For example, an IT service such as the ERP system may involve several hundred hardware, software, and network components collectively delivering the service to users. A failure in even one of those hundreds of components can stop the entire service.

Here are the most common causes of operational failures:

- Power failure
- Software failure
- Hardware failure
- Network failure (hardware or software for network system)
- Integration systems failures (interplay between systems)
- Software and hardware glitches (bugs)
- Data loss
- Data corruption

- Cybersecurity incidents
- Incompatibility between two systems due to upgrade or patching

Costs associated with IT service interruptions due to these types of incidents can run into hundreds or thousands of dollars a month for a big, global company. All these risks require deliberate planning and mitigation strategies, including lots of redundancies in the infrastructure. The most common mitigation strategies for such operational risks include:

- Redundancies—
  - Hardware or software clustering where a system has a pair of devices with one active while the other is passive and can be "failed over" in case the primary node fails.
  - Pooling—services are delivered with a pool of resources (servers) so that the load is distributed and the failure of one node does not affect the whole service.
- Backups—Periodic backup snapshots of data and software configuration taken to mitigate the risks of data loss or data corruption. In the event of data loss or data corruption, one can revert to the most recent snapshot saved and resume services.
- Electric power redundancies—
  - Dual power supplies to all hardware, each rack, and the whole data center. These redundancies allow us to tolerate a failure of one circuit or grid without interrupting the end service.
  - Uninterruptible power supply (UPS)—This is an auxiliary power supply (a big battery) that temporarily extends power to IT hardware in case of power grid failure. However, UPSs are mostly used for the short period (a few seconds to a few minutes) while you transition from the power grid to generators.
  - Generators provide power to the data center when the power grid is down for an extended period. These can run for a long time as long as you supply the fuel.

With such redundancies in your IT environment, you need to invest proportionately in additional human resources for monitoring these systems round the clock and a maintenance crew to act upon any incidents as well as perform preventive maintenance.

Besides the internal costs of redundant hardware, software, and human resources, companies also have costly third-party maintenance contracts. Such contracts are primarily with software or hardware vendors who then provide expert help during outages. Despite having large teams to manage IT systems, no IT team members can be experts in troubleshooting every piece of software or hardware, and they will often have to depend on expert help from the vendor's engineers.

It's no surprise that all these things cost a lot of money. Essentially, the primary cost of delivering an IT service is not very high. However, the total cost of delivering the IT service with the highest level of availability and reliability goes up exponentially. If a company decides to run an IT operation without investing adequately in redundant infrastructure or the workforce and dedicated crew required to maintain it, IT services can be delivered inexpensively. However, the services will be prone to regular outages, which in turn could translate to the loss of revenue/customers. Sometimes it's not that easy to quantify the effect in real dollars of service interruptions. However, the costs are real, and they can hurt productivity and morale. It's crucial for users to have full confidence in IT systems all the time.

It may come as a surprise, but the cost of owning and managing the bare necessities without redundancies can be as little as a third or less of the normal cost. The bulk of the IT budget is investment in all the necessary redundancies and the monitoring and maintenance workforce. All those costs can contribute to the remaining two-thirds of the total cost.

Compliance risks

Every company has at least a few regulations with which they have to comply. Regulations affecting IT systems and operations are mostly industry-specific. Therefore, CIOs must understand the rules governing the company they work for and what IT needs to do to comply with those regulations.

If you are the CIO of a global company with worldwide operations, then your corporate structure most likely has lots of local, country-specific legal corporate entities. Each of these entities must abide by local regulations. Failure to comply can be devastating to the company's future, including the possibility of completely shutting down the business for good.

Here is a set of typical compliance risks CIOs must understand. This list is by no means exhaustive.

Country-specific regulations (labor laws, financial reporting, taxation)

- Securities and Exchange Commission regulations (or equivalent in other countries)
- Insider trading regulations
- Sarbanes-Oxley Act (or equivalent)
- Payment card industry (PCI) compliance
- HIPPA (Health Insurance Portability and Accountability Act) compliance
- ITAR (international traffic in arms regulations) compliance
- Safety regulations (OSHA—Occupational Safety and Health Administration)
- Privacy regulations

Most of these regulations require annual audits and certifications by third-party auditors. All these regulations affect how we manage IT infrastructure, services, and the controls we put in place to ensure compliance.

These regulations are quite elaborate and require IT experts who specialize in the given regulations. CIOs are not expected to be experts on all the details of every regulation, but they are responsible for understanding how these regulations affect the organizations they serve. They also must understand precisely how these regulations affect their teams and technology.

These regulations affect how we manage IT operations and which IT general controls (ITGC) we implement to ensure compliance. Aspect of ITGCs and IT service management cover a wide array of tasks, including physical and logical access to the network and critical systems, role-based security, physical security, cybersecurity, backups, data security, privacy protections, asset management, incident response, disaster recovery, business continuity, and so on.

Many of these regulations are relatively complex and can be very difficult to understand. Also, few explicitly spell out which aspect of the regulation is IT's responsibility. You will have to interpret the rules to ensure compliance.

Luckily, even though all these regulations have IT aspects, there can be many similarities between regulations. As such, if you run your IT shop on a robust industry-accepted framework like ITIL (Information Technology Infrastructure Library), it's not that difficult to ensure compliance with regulations.

Disaster recovery and business continuity risks

Perils in this category are typically large-scale incidents that pose a significant threat to companywide systems. Risks in this category include disasters that can bring your whole IT infrastructure (data centers, network, office buildings) down, bringing services to a screeching halt.

Many of the operational risks we discussed earlier can affect the whole system, creating system-wide outages, such as power failures or cyber incidents. However, there are some rare risks, such as earthquakes, flooding, fire, windstorms, arson, and so on. Such disasters can damage the entire IT infrastructure and delivery network, thereby affecting services.

Such disasters can be considered operational risks but at a much larger magnitude. The risks covered in this category are not as routine as the other type of failures we discussed in the operational risks category, but their scale can be enormous, and the consequences could be much worse and long-lasting.

In a nutshell, this risk category focuses on how well you can sustain operations during a major disaster and how fast you can recover from a catastrophe. The second aspect of this risk category focuses on ensuring continuity of business operations after disaster strikes. Here are some of the common perils that can affect the complete system.

- Data center fire
- Physical damage due to earthquake, flooding, windstorm
- Physical destruction due to war, arson, accident
- Water damage in the data center

Any of these perils can shut down IT infrastructure, thereby affecting all IT services. Mitigation strategies include prevention strategies and response and recovery strategies. Obviously, lots of planning is done to be ready to recover from any disaster, but substantial energy and cost also go into preventing or at least minimizing the effects of these risks.

All data centers are equipped with multiple protections against such risks and their effects. The more you focus on preventing disasters, the less you will have to depend on your recovery mechanisms.

For fire, protection mechanisms include encasing data centers in robust, fireproof walls and ceilings and fire suppression mechanisms.

For flooding, planning goes into locating data centers ideally so there is no water flow above, below, or around the data center. Also, there are many mechanisms in place to prevent water damage to hardware in the racks.

There are no prevention methods for earthquakes, but in countries like Japan, where earthquakes are frequent, specially designed features are included in data centers. For example, they put springs under data center flooring or racks to absorb vibrations caused by earthquakes so they don't damage the servers inside the racks.

If, despite all the prevention mechanisms, disasters do strike, one must be well prepared for recovery. The key is recovering as smoothly and as quickly as possible. You design your recovery effort based on risk tolerance and how mission-critical your operation is. Two key parameters to ascertain and understand are: How long can the function afford to be down (the total outage of service measured in Recovery Time Objective—RTO), and how much data/transaction loss can you afford (measured by Recovery Point Objective—RPO)?

If the answer to both questions is *zero*, then you are dealing with a near-impossible scenario. However, if you ask stakeholders, they would say they can't afford any data loss or system outages whatsoever, and from their perspective, this may be true. No one can really afford to stop work or lose data. But it is nearly impossible and exorbitantly expensive to even attempt to meet such expectations. The higher the level of preparedness your operation needs, the higher the costs. Before you finalize your critical parameters, ensure you know what's really needed and what you can afford. Once you put a dollar value on accomplishing these objectives, CEOs and CFOs can make informed decisions on the level of risk they are willing to accept.

Irrespective of your RTO and RPO parameters, traditionally, the two most common recovery strategies have been backups and off-site replication. Lately, recovery strategies have been transitioning to Cloud-based systems, altogether eliminating the need for backup or second-site replication. Let's review all these three recovery strategies:

Data and system backups: This is a most common method of preparing for recovering from major disasters. All software and hardware systems and data are backed up and stored somewhere outside of the primary data center. Traditionally, data is backed up to tape drives, but now Cloud backup is a desirable option. Much planning goes into what to back up, how often to take backup snapshots, how to store the backed-up data, how long to retain each snapshot, where to store it, and how to recover the data when needed. While tape backups have been the gold standard so far, they are rife with disadvantages, such as loss of tapes, lack of encryption, third-party handling, poor tape quality, expensive tape libraries, and tape backup software. Cloud backups have the potential to solve many of these problems and provide much more reliable and safer backups almost instantaneously. I anticipate tape backups will vanish from IT infrastructure completely in the next decade or so.

However, merely backing up data does not necessarily mean you can quickly resume business operations after a disastrous event. Data backup is necessary but insufficient from a business continuity perspective. In a real recovery scenario, all you can ensure is that you have the latest data and systems backup somewhere outside the primary data center. You would still have to bring that data to another data center, procure and set up new hardware and software to the original configurations, restore your backed-up data, and finally, make network connections to the new data center so business operations can resume.

Depending on the scale of recovery, all these steps can take anywhere from weeks to months or even multiple quarters. If that means business operations will have to be shut down during the recovery period, that is an unacceptable level of preparedness. That's why most businesses go to the next level of readiness and establish secondary data centers as a mirror image of the primary data center, so all services can be transferred in case of a major disaster at the primary data center.

System replication to the secondary data center: This is the next level of preparedness, in which all systems, hardware, software, network, data storage, etc. are mirrored at a separate data center. This replication essentially doubles the IT investment needed because you are duplicating every aspect of your IT infrastructure. A fully mirrored and replicated data center is the ultimate redundancy.

If your business operation cannot afford system outages, this is your only viable option. Despite the high cost, replication is often easily justified, since the loss of even one day's revenue may be more than the cost of investing in a secondary data center. This configuration adds tremendous complexity to IT infrastructure because every component needs to be replicated in real time and kept ready at all times at another location.

Traditionally, this has been achieved through exact, mirror copies of data center infrastructure, but now more and more is possible using the Cloud. If companies are exploring the Cloud as an option for data backup, the same system can be further exploited in the realm of disaster recovery operations. This way, two efforts can be consolidated to achieve the business continuity goal.

Cloud transition: If you can transition from on-premise systems to a public, cloud-based service, then you don't really have to worry about backup and disaster recovery replication. This is true only if you transition to a public cloud provider that enables similar services in a multi-tenant model so your data is stored along with hundreds of other customers' data. The Cloud provider is taking ownership of doing backups and replication to a secondary site and ensuring the service level objectives they are contractually obligated to maintain.

A simple example is a big global company hosting its email in different regions may use dozens of servers and software instances on-site when you combine all the instances for production primary, production secondary, development, quality assurance (QA) and testing, backup, and replication. By switching to a publicly available service such as Microsoft Office 365 or Google G Suite, you can not only eliminate all this hardware, software, and the associated maintenance, but also get better guarantees on backups and disaster recovery preparedness than what your internal IT teams could provide. The best thing about this transition is that it actually reduces IT costs substantially.

This same scenario is now true for most commercially available software systems. Hardly any software vendors exist that do not provide Cloud-based Software as a Service (SaaS) subscriptions. Increasingly, this Cloud transition is becoming a viable and desirable alternative for backups and disaster recovery, even for custom applications, backbone systems, storage with Infrastructure as a Service (IaaS), or Platform as a Service (PaaS). All are just different flavors of the Cloud business model focusing on various aspects of IT infrastructure.

This third recovery strategy—transitioning to the Cloud for disaster recovery preparedness—is the most common strategy today and will soon become the only viable strategy for the bulk of IT infrastructure.

Cybersecurity risks

If you look at the last decade, cybersecurity is arguably the most significant IT risk for any company. This risk far outpaces any other risk categories we have discussed. It's big in scale, complex in scope, and can have devastating results for any company. That's why all CIO board presentations lately have been heavily focused on the state of cybersecurity and preparedness. There is too much at stake, and hence, audit committees, whose primary charter is risk governance, are laser-focused on this issue. All my board presentations or interactions with board members over the last decade have been overwhelmingly focused on cybersecurity efforts, with very little time spent on digital transformation or other strategic opportunities for IT.

The purpose of our discussion on this topic is not to provide a comprehensive guide for how best to manage cybersecurity risks but to appreciate the magnitude of the risks. Also, we want to understand what CIOs must be aware of and how they should navigate these risks, more from a business perspective than just the technical perspective.

In the past, you may not have heard of CEOs or even CIOs getting fired because of IT risks, but that's not the case when it comes to cybersecurity incidents. On the contrary, you will see that CEO and CIO accountability is paramount when it comes to cybersecurity. It's because the risk and consequences are unparalleled. The implications of a security breach can be more devastating than any other disaster or fraudulent dealings.

Unfortunately, because cybersecurity risks are continually evolving, and new types of incidents are coming to light every other day, unfortunately, much confusion exists among company executives about the exact nature of cyber risks and how they affect their company. The situation is, regrettably, amplified by massive propaganda by IT vendors, auditors, media, high-end consultants, and industry forums. A recent Gartner forecast estimated security spending at $96 billion in 2018 alone, and it is expected to rise over the next few years. I wouldn't trivialize the risk, but there is a strong need for buyers to understand the nature and scope of cyber risks before buying a lot of tools and services. If you don't know the precise nature of the problem (risk) you are solving, then you don't know whether your security investments are helping or hurting you.

Cybersecurity risks are so diverse and so deep that the defense used by one company may be much different from that needed at another company, even in the same industry. Cybersecurity is indeed unique to every company. There are some common threats and patterns, but the risk tolerance for each company is very different, and therefore, mitigation strategies must be unique to precisely fit the risk on hand.

A unique challenge for CIOs is not only to understand the risks and develop a cybersecurity program, but to educate c-suite executives, the board of directors, and auditors on risks and mitigation strategies. It takes special skills to clarify the problem and ensure their perceptions and assumptions about the cybersecurity risk are based on facts. Everyone's understanding of cybersecurity risks and mitigation is vastly different. It is the CIO's job to educate and get buy-in to ensure stakeholders are on board with your assessment of the risks and your mitigation strategy. This is where the business acumen supporting technical skills comes into the picture. Remember, risk management is a business problem, not a technical one. As with any business decisions, a great deal of uncertainty exists, and those decisions must be made within the overall context of your company's mission, culture, and risk tolerance.

Even if the risks for two companies are precisely the same, their mitigation strategies and investments could be vastly different because of varying risk tolerances. It is similar to having different levels of liability insurance even though the risks for all may be the same.

A most common assumption by all stakeholders is that cybersecurity is 100 percent the CIO's responsibility. Nothing can be further from the truth, and CIOs must rise above this perception and educate everyone that cybersecurity is an enterprise-wide risk, not just an IT risk. Yes, CIOs are responsible for establishing technical defense mechanisms, but most cyber incidents are traceable by people's actions, policies/practices, company culture, security spending levels, and company's risk tolerance. Technical defenses are only a portion of a comprehensive cybersecurity risk mitigation plan.

For example, CIOs can devise the best cybersecurity policies and defense mechanisms, but if they interfere with user productivity and business efficiency, most policies will be breached. As we know, it's human nature to be as efficient and productive as possible, and risks are a secondary concern until they become real. CIOs may not get much support for their policies if the company's overall culture doesn't appreciate cybersecurity risk or promote user compliance with such policies even when they get in the way of production.

Another factor that complicates matters is the continually changing landscape of cybersecurity threats and defense mechanisms. It is, by far, the fastest changing landscape in information technology. The scope of cybersecurity threats and defense changes very quickly and will continue to evolve at this rate for decades to come.

Given the constant evolution of threats, confusion among stakeholders, panic among some, lack of clear strategy, and massive propaganda from external sources, how should CIOs address this risk effectively? Here is a high-level approach that CIOs can use.

1. Understand the threat.
To begin with, I recommend CIOs set aside time every month to learn about and understand developments in cybersecurity. You have to make an extra effort to stay current on threats and mitigation tools. At the very

least, understand what the most common cyber threats are, their frequency, and the likelihood they will affect your company. Also, try to assess *how* those threats could affect your company.

The most common cyber threats are:

- Generic mass hacking
- Advanced persistent threats (APT)—usually specific threats by state actors
- Malware attacks—viruses, worms, ransomware
- Insider threats
- Poor behaviors among insiders

The typical impacts of these cyber threats on businesses include:

- Money theft—especially from financial institutions
- Ransom
- Identity theft
- Data manipulation with mal-intent
- Business disruption
- Intellectual property theft
- Privacy regulations breach
- Business reputation and credibility attacks
- Customer information loss

Before you get any further, spend time determining the scope of these risks and their effect on your company.

2. Develop unique risk profile.

This is, by far, the most crucial step in figuring out which threats are real for your company. It's important to define which you should address. It also captures your risk tolerance, which will guide you in developing a custom cybersecurity program.

Without this critical step, you will most likely have a very vague and ineffective security program that may or may not address your real risks.

Remember, when it comes to cybersecurity, unfortunately, no one standard roadmap fits all companies. Every cybersecurity program must be custom-made to address your specific risks and tolerance levels. This is where you sort out the noise from the real risks and focus on those.

Defining your company's risk profile is not an easy task. It can best be done by professionals trained in this exercise. If you don't have a chief information security officer (CISO), hire one. If you can't afford a full-time, permanent CISO, you can hire expert consultants on a project basis. CISOs conduct a formal assessment from which they develop your risk profile. They will most likely use one of the standard industry frameworks based on NIST 800 or SANS 20 or ISO 27000.

Through this formal assessment, CISOs or expert consultants can determine which types of cyber risks affect your company and which ones don't. The first aspect of such evaluation is risk classification based on likelihood and business impact. You can classify all cyber threats as low, medium, or high based on likelihood and impact scales. If you plot all cyber threats on a three-by-three matrix of likelihood and impact, it can help you figure out which threats are most severe and should be your first focus.

The second aspect of this assessment is to understand your company's risk tolerance. Some entrepreneurial CEOs may indeed be more comfortable with risks if they are more concerned with the cost of mitigating risks than the resulting costs of a security breach.

The result of such a thorough assessment would be a comprehensive cybersecurity program addressing all major risks and outlining specific projects required for doing just that.

3. Develop and execute the cybersecurity program.

Based on the assessment, risk profile, and framework you choose, a comprehensive cybersecurity program can be developed and implemented. Do understand that these programs are neither trivial nor quick. In most cases, it takes one to three years to establish the basic cybersecurity process. Also, recognize that *cybersecurity is a race without a finish line.*

Yes, there are plenty of markers along the way but expect to be in this race forever. There is the initial implementation to establish a baseline, and then you transition to maintenance mode with monitoring and continuous enhancements to the cybersecurity programs.

Here are the essential elements of any cybersecurity program:

- A cybersecurity steering committee to get all key stakeholders on the same page
- Well-defined policies that articulate expected behavior from users and IT teams
- Well-defined processes, especially related to threat detection, incident response, and recovery.
- A prioritized list of projects based on the risk assessment. Such lists would be the bulk of your cybersecurity program. These can easily involve dozens of projects using ten to twenty different defense technologies that need to be procured, installed, configured, and used. These may include any or all the elements listed below.
  - Advanced firewalls to develop sophisticated traffic controls
  - Email protection systems for spam, malware, ransomware, phishing
  - Password vault system for system administrators and users
  - Endpoint clients for anti-virus, anti-spam, anti-malware protection
  - Identity and access management (IAM) systems
  - Access control technologies such as Active Directory or equivalent, single sign on (SSO), multi-factor authentication
  - Network reconfiguration and topology to minimize entry and exit points
  - Network local area network (LAN) and wide area network (WAN) re-architecture to isolate high-risk areas and control access

- Wireless network re-architecture and control mechanisms
- Network demilitarized zone (DMZ) configuration to tightly control the boundaries
- Encryption technologies for hard disks, email, websites, data storage systems, databases, file transport systems, and network circuits (data encryption is needed both when data is at-rest [stored] in any system or while in transit inside or outside your company network.)
- Data storage device controls to block the use of USB, CD, DVD, or cloud storage systems
- Web surfing and access controls to monitor user actions on the Internet and adhere to policies for access to their private email, cloud storage systems, and so on
- Mobile device management systems to control access and privileges from mobile devices
- System and network hardening to ensure tight controls on hardware, software, and network configuration
- Network asset discovery systems to inventory all the devices on your network
- Vulnerability scanning and management systems
- Patching systems to keep all hardware and software up to date, at least for critical and high impact patches
- Remote software and patch delivery systems
- Data loss prevention (DLP) and digital rights management (DRM) systems where advanced controls are required for managing intellectual property (IP) use and transmission
- Secure printing and faxing solutions with encryption, if needed
- Security incident and event management (SIEM) systems to continually monitor all activity to detect threats and respond promptly (SIEM is a critical defense mechanism without which all the defenses deployed may be ineffective.)

- Communication of cybersecurity program to all stakeholders, users, company owners/executives, customers, board members, auditors, and suppliers.
- Continuous education and training of end users. Cybersecurity is something that must be continuously on your radar, developing a culture of constant vigilance.

Cybersecurity is a race without a finish line. Expect to be part of this journey for a long time.

All the key risk categories we discussed here—operational, compliance, disaster recovery, and cybersecurity—constitute the major risk focus that CIOs must ensure. As we discussed, CIOs can't lose sight of risk management, no matter how laser-focused they are on the business value delivery aspect of their job. However, understanding the scope of these risks and the mitigation strategies helps CIOs ensure that any of the risks don't put you in a wrong spot when you least expect it.

By now, we have covered two most important aspects of the perfect imbalance equation—business value and risk management. If CIOs do these two aspects of their job right, they would be considered successful in most aspects. Now we will focus on the third element of this equation: the IT cost management. The purpose of discussing this section after the business value and risk is to recognize that the cost aspect is of lesser importance than the other two factors. Nonetheless, as we will discuss in the next chapter, it does drive significant value to the business so it is something CIOs shouldn't ignore.

Part IV

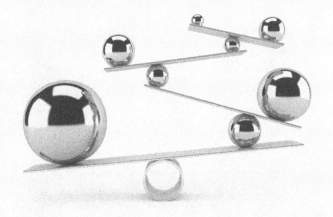

The Cost Equation

CHAPTER 11

Understanding IT Costs

Where does all the money really go?

Let's look at the IT cost equation. Managing costs has always been one of the key priorities for CEOs and CFOs, and therefore, all CIOs. Most companies do an excellent job of managing costs; however, I have seen the same traps driving up costs time and again.

Before we get into the various strategies for effectively managing IT costs, let's look at a typical IT cost breakdown. Variation exists from company to company and industry to industry, but most IT cost breakdowns would look something like the following:

Category	% of Total IT Cost

Labor
    Employee
    Contractors/Consultants
	30%

Depreciation	20%

Hardware & Software
    Expensed hardware/software
    Software Maintenance
    Hardware Maintenance
    Cloud Subscriptions
	35%

Telecommunications & Networks	10%
Everything else	5%
Total	**100%**

Table 11-1: IT Cost Breakdown

We will look at all of the above categories in detail, what each includes, the key contributing factors, the pitfalls, and most importantly, specific actions you can take to optimize these costs. You can merely rank all these cost categories from largest to smallest and work on optimizing expenses in that order. However, unfortunately, not all categories have similar potential for cost reductions. Some have many opportunities while others have very few.

Here is a simple prioritization technique that will help you focus on the right things and in the right order: Classify all the cost categories in a two by two matrix based on cost and value.

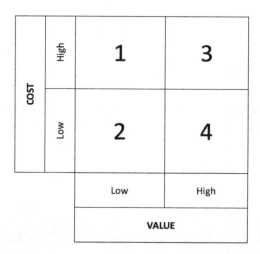

Figure 11-1: IT Value – Cost Matrix

Classifying categories on a cost scale is easy, but it is harder to do on a value scale. Value is a lot more critical and subjective. As a CIO, you would know which software and hardware systems are essential for running your day-to-day business. We often call those mission-critical systems. These systems can stop daily operations if they experience outages. Day-to-day operations include your core business—manufacturing, teaching, broadcasting, selling online, hospitality, healthcare, and so on. Mission-critical activities also include essential support services needed for your core business, such as taking orders, processing orders, scheduling, shipping, billing, or cash collection.

In other words, if you have a system that can interfere with revenue, profits, or customer satisfaction, it should be considered a high-value, mission-critical system.

The rest can be classified as low-value systems that are required but not critical, where you can afford some poor performance. Such systems may include applications for overhead or support functions. Please note, the users in these areas would argue that their system is mission critical. You, as CIO, must prioritize these areas with a CEO hat on—classify them the way your CEO would classify them. We will discuss this "thinking and acting like a CEO" in detail in future sections of this book.

Key cost-optimization strategies

Once you classify all the cost categories into these four quadrants, your prioritization is simplified. You can focus on categories in quadrant one and then move to quadrant two, then to three, and finally, to quadrant four. Here are the three most common cost-optimization strategies:

- Cost elimination
- Cost arbitration—replacement with better and cheaper options
- Negotiation of favorable terms

You can use one or more of these strategies for any cost elements. In most cases, you would end up using more than one strategy.

Cost elimination

Elimination is the best form of cost reduction. If you are inheriting an IT operation with a long history, you may come across many items that continue to add cost while providing little to no value. In some cases, especially with renewals, no one can articulate the business rationale for spending that money. Their best answer could be, "Because we have been doing this for a long time." That answer, by itself, is certainly not a business case.

Cost components that fall in the low-value category are good candidates
for cost elimination as a first strategy. Costs like hardware maintenance on
desktops, laptops, printers, peripherals, or access switches are best examples of candidates for such a strategy. There are also expenses like third-party monitoring and alerting, which can cost a lot of money, but all they do
is inform your administrator there is a problem. They don't resolve issues.

You will also find such expenses in many software maintenance contracts,
which may have never been used, but you still pay for them every year.
Most such expenses, while they may look good on paper, bring little value.

Depending on how well IT spending has been managed previously, you
may be able to quickly cut 5-10 percent of your total cost without reducing services.

Cost arbitrage—replace with something better and cheaper

If you are not able to eliminate the cost of specific line items, the next best
thing is to find a cheaper alternative. Given the pace of change in technology and the industry's competitive nature, many IT components become
obsolete in three to five years. If you provide rewards and recognition
for teams/team members who present opportunities for replacing existing solutions with better and/or cheaper ones, you will be surprised how
many solutions come forward.

You can find opportunities to use this strategy for almost any IT costs.
Here are just a few examples:

- Replace high-end laptops with moderate ones (much of the
  power built into these machines may not be used or realized
  by users).
- Replace original equipment manufacturer (OEM) hardware
  warranties with third-party maintenance contracts.
- Replace expensive private circuits with next generation, soft-
  ware-defined wide area network (SDWAN) with plain internet circuits.

- Replace tape backups with cloud backups.
- Replace higher-cost vendors with others who can meet the same specifications on commodities—laptops, desktops, peripherals, printers, productivity tools, or network circuits.

Negotiate favorable terms

This is your last cost-optimization strategy, and you use it where you know a specific service adds considerable value but also costs a lot of money. High costs for value-added systems/equipment is natural. It's also common to see the most expensive systems bringing the most value to your business. Every company has several big-ticket items in their IT budget that they can't do without but also represent a significant drain on your budget.

Such high-value, high-cost items include things like annual maintenance on your major enterprise systems like ERP, manufacturing execution systems (MES), or e-commerce systems, hardware maintenance on mission-critical systems, long-term consultants in core competency areas, wide area network circuits, telecom circuits, and many more like these. In most cases, replacing these with another viable service is nearly impossible and can take a long time.

In such cases, the best you can do is negotiate better terms—financial or non-financial—that can help you optimize the costs. For example, you can downgrade from premier support to standard business hours support or from platinum support to silver support. You can also reduce the scope of assistance to only the production environment instead of covering the whole development and QA environments as well. If you have a lot of unused software you are paying annual maintenance on, you can negotiate a pause for a few years or remove the support for unused portions altogether.

These three broad cost-optimization strategies are generic in nature. In the next few chapters, we will discuss in detail how to apply these strategies to optimize costs in each category and which strategies work best for each cost category.

CHAPTER 12

So How Do We Control These Costs?

Can one technique work for managing all costs?

The cost-optimization strategies we have discussed so far are widely used, but the way they can be applied to each cost category is entirely different. Every cost category has its own unique set of dynamics and pitfalls and, therefore, requires different cost-optimization techniques within these broad strategies.

This chapter is devoted to discussing cost categories in great detail, including what the category includes and any special dynamics or pitfalls associated. Most importantly, we will then review the specific actions you can take to manage these costs.

Cost-optimization exercises can take anywhere from one to three years and depend significantly on understanding the costs in detail and analyzing them to figure out proper actions. At the end of this cost-optimization exercise, you may be able to generate a total savings of 10-30 percent of your overall IT budget. Depending on the size of your budget, this could translate into millions or even tens of millions of dollars annually.

1. Labor cost
Labor cost includes direct and indirect costs associated with IT personnel. This is, by far, the most high value-added cost category. It includes cost for full-time employees and outsourced, contract labor.

All IT departments have both pools to a varying degree. Both these labor pools have different value propositions concerning cost and flexibility. They also have different challenges associated with optimizing the costs and require different techniques to manage those effectively.

1.1 Employee labor cost
Approximately 15-20 percent of total IT cost
Reduction potential: Low short-term but could be moderate long-term
Cost-Value quadrant: 3

Employee labor cost is most likely to be either your number one or number two cost category, irrespective of your company's size or industry. It also has less potential for cost reduction than many other areas we will discuss.

Labor cost is the total expense of employee direct and indirect compensation, such as payroll, taxes, and benefits. Most of these costs are out of the CIO's control. They are driven by market supply and demand, labor regulations, and the company's overall HR policies.

There aren't many quick yet logical actions you can take to reduce expenses in this category unless you reduce your workforce. Of course, if companies lay off their associates to reduce costs, they are taking short-term steps that may be detrimental to IT services but may be essential for company survival. Any actions one can take in optimizing this expense category would be long-term and strategic in nature. There is no short-term cost benefit, unless you reduce your workforce.

However, CIOs can do a good job strategically by proactively managing this expense, ensuring sustainable IT services while also providing necessary flexibility, which, in turn, helps you navigate the bumps along the way. Strategic considerations relate to the following set of questions:

- What's your talent-sourcing strategy? How do you determine whether a role should be filled by an employee or contracted out?

- Does this position meet a short-term or long-term need? Will you need someone to do this job for an extended period?
- Will this person make medium- to long-term decisions or tactical, day-to-day decisions?
- Is this role related to your business' core competency? Or is it less critical?
- Does long-term retention matter from a continuity perspective?
- What's the desired employee to contractor ratio for your company? This applies when there is such a directive from HR.
- How hard is it to fill the position? Is there a glut of qualified applicants?
- How long does it take to fill the position and bring the new person up to speed in case of turnover?

If you haven't defined a thorough talent-sourcing strategy, you should consider doing a simple, three-way classification of all the roles in your department to determine whether a full-time, in-house employee is needed or the role can be contracted out to an external service provider.

	Criteria	Example Roles
I	• Key leadership positions required to define and execute strategies • Key director roles requiring extensive business process and company culture knowledge • Roles related to your core competency • Roles that are critical long-term • Roles that primarily make mid- to long-term decisions • Positions making huge monetary decisions	• CIO and key direct reports • Senior leadership roles, IT area owners • Business analysts • Senior system administrators • Business function liaisons
II	• Roles that are critical in the short-term but can be managed long-term with little effect • Roles in short supply at a hiring location • Roles that directly contribute to IT service delivery • Roles that make mid-term decisions related to processes and services • Roles that have gray areas and are not as prescriptive	• Solution architects • Enterprise architecture • Systems analysts • Team leads
III	• Roles that are easy to find where supply exceeds demand • Roles that are generic in nature and do not need strong domain expertise • Easy-to-do knowledge transfer from one person to another • Roles that have low to moderate short-term impact but can be easily absorbed by other skills • Roles that are prescriptive and allow for someone to be trained using knowledge transfer books	• Software testing/QA • Backend support • System administration • Development • 24/7 Monitoring • Level 1 support

Table 12-1: Talent-Sourcing Strategy

The classification above allows you to define a granular sourcing strategy that makes sense for each category. The strategy can be straightforward. Type I roles must be filled with full-time employees while type III roles can be contracted to an external service provider. However, type II roles are a mix and can go either way, but attempts should be made to keep them in the first category.

The effect of type I & II roles on the success of your IT operations is very high compared to type III roles. However, please note that you need all the roles to be able to deliver your services effectively. Do not assume you can eliminate type III roles and still run the IT operation. That's not possible.

Once you design your organization, equally important process is active and continuous talent management. It takes constant focus and a hands-on approach to ensure that all our human resources are actively contributing to our short- and long-term goals.

Many books have been written about talent management. I am neither an expert nor a coach in this area. I am sure your HR department has very well-defined talent management training and performance-management processes. You must depend on those processes to actively manage the talent in IT. However, recognize that IT talent management is unique, and some special considerations are needed in ensuring low cost and high efficiency in your labor pool. We will discuss unique aspects of IT talent management in a later section of this book focusing on the essential CIO skills.

1.2 Long-term consultants/contractors
Approximate 10-15 percent of total IT cost
Reduction potential: 5-10 percent of this category's total
Cost-Value quadrant: 1

Most CIOs realize this is a big expense category. Nonetheless, this expense continues to grow as a percent of total IT budgets. Let's first understand what this includes and how we got here.

It wasn't that long ago that all IT associates were full-time employees. However, given the fast pace of change in the IT industry, skills become obsolete quickly. That fast pace and the associated changes in the skills needed make it difficult to keep up with technology if we have employees whose skills aren't keeping pace with the industry. Companies find themselves in a bind where they have surplus skills and capacity in one IT area while acutely lacking skills in other areas.

The same pace of required skill changes also drove fragmentation and specialization. Associates became experts in a niche area. Long gone are the days when any IT administrator could pretty much manage all types of hardware or systems analysts could handle all types of software. There is an even greater degree of specialization within each software or hardware technology. For example, a generic ERP system like SAP requires a multitude of skills to keep it together, such as business analyst, functional analyst, technical analyst, ABAP developer, integration lead, basis administrator, and database administrator.

In IT, every specialized skill comes with an expiration date not far in the future. That quick expiration date phenomenon, plus an ever-rising demand for new skills, quickly creates a mismatch of skills, which, in turn, discourages employers from hiring full-time staff and encourages them to hire contractors. However, a difference exists between getting consulting expertise help to fill a short-term need versus using contractors to augment staff over a long period.

Many companies use contract labor from external service providers, which makes sense for various reasons discussed above, fully knowing it comes at a premium. Over time, this business practice can create a huge cost burden such that a large chunk of money is spent on expensive, long-term consultants each year.

Please realize that contractors and consultants also add equal or even more value and are essential for delivering IT services. Unlike employees, the skills external contractors/consultants possess are always current. They keep their skills up to date so they are always marketable. Usually, most companies have a mix of employees and contract labor in their IT workforce.

Here are some common techniques to optimize this expense category:

- Define your sourcing strategy by skill and role. Define what's long-term vs. short-term, critical vs. secondary, and classify them into whether an employee, long-term contractor, short-term contractor, or outsourced service model is right for each of those roles.
- Define your need's duration. If you need someone with a particular skill for more than twenty-four months, hire an employee, not a contractor.
- Define the results you need, don't just hire a person's time. This is also called Managed Service where you hold the third party accountable for delivering the required results. This is possible for standard and well-defined services but not suited as well for complicated development or implementation projects.

2. Depreciation costs
Approximately 20-25 percent of total IT cost
Reduction potential: 5-7 percent of this category's total over time
Cost-Value quadrant: 3

Not that long ago, depreciation costs used to be the biggest or second biggest expense category in IT budgets. However, the recent rise in cloud computing is drastically shifting IT spending from capital expenditure (Capex) to operating expenditure (Opex).

Like payroll costs, this category does not have any quick actions for reducing costs immediately. However, several strategies could affect the amount of depreciation over three to five years.

Let's first understand the typical depreciation expenses in IT budgets. As you may know, companies can capitalize many big-ticket items and can spread the cost over time. Although a lot of cash is spent upfront, from a financial accounting perspective, the cost is spread over time. CIOs only have influence over depreciation cost when it comes to selecting equipment or software system. Once the money is spent, an item's expense is set in stone and will remain on your accounting books until the end of the depreciation schedule.

All companies have capitalization rules and guidelines for what can and cannot be capitalized and the period of depreciation for various assets. Many of these rules are driven by generally acceptable accounting principles (GAAP) guidelines, but few aspects are determined by company management based on their risk threshold.

Capitalization is buying a tangible asset that is useful for multiple years, such as major hardware or software purchases or buying a building. Initial cost can also include the cost associated with "turning on" that asset, which, in the case of IT systems, means the cost of implementation. However, there are rules for which implementation costs can be capitalized and which ones can't.

Three major trends over the last ten to fifteen years are reducing depreciable expenses in IT budgets:

- Falling cost of IT assets
- Shrinking lifespan of IT assets due to fast technological improvements
- Transitioning to cloud computing

Remember the old days of major ERP projects costing tens of millions of dollars and lasting several years? Or the cost of building major data centers and all the peripheral systems needed to operate them? Those were big capital expenses that remained on the accounting books for several years. In the case of the data center, a physical asset, that Capex could even be spread out over the course of up to thirty years.

Now, even big ERP projects are done in small phases and often cost only hundreds of thousands of dollars. They are typically turned on in less than a year and are kept on the books for just three to five years because that ERP will be old and ready for a significant upgrade in five years.

The most significant catalyst in driving depreciation costs down has been the transition to cloud computing, both on the software side (software as a service - SaaS) as well as infrastructure or platform as a service (IaaS, PaaS).

By the very nature of the cloud computing business model, customers don't own any assets. They get rights to use the assets owned and managed by the vendor on the vendor's own premises (metaphorically described as the Cloud). Even though customers may end up spending a lot more money using that service over a long period, none of that can be capitalized. Because you don't pay anything upfront (pay as you go) and you don't own anything, there is no asset to depreciate, just a service.

This transformation is not necessarily reducing IT costs but moving them from the capital spending (depreciation) bucket to the operating expense bucket. However, a sizable portion of your IT budget is likely still in this category. What actions can you take to reduce such expense—albeit slowly and over a long period?

Remember, you only have one opportunity to influence this cost—at the time of initial procurement and provisioning. Here are three key steps worth following rigorously in all capital spending decisions.

- **Business case:** Is there a sound business case for this spending?
- **Alignment:** Is this well aligned with top-level stakeholders and their mission?
- **Total Cost of Ownership (TCO):** Is total cost understood at a detailed level and over the depreciation period?

Many capital spending proposals can be turned down if the business case or alignment to the mission are not well articulated. Also, be aware that business cases must be factual and data-driven versus opinion-driven.

In the IT world, there are two types of projects: department-driven and IT-driven for the company's overall benefit.

In both types of projects, as CIO, you will often have to wade through flimsy business cases. If the CIO doesn't have a grasp on technology or business processes, it's not that difficult to convince them to spend money. Here are some examples of business case justifications I have heard for both types of projects. Some may be correct, while many can be very flimsy and in need of more in-depth evaluation.

Information technology-driven projects

- This hardware/software is very old.
- It's no longer supported.
- The company that made it doesn't exist anymore.
- It's very old technology.
- It's very slow.
- It's not very stable; we've had many incident reports recently.
- It's not the latest technology.
- We don't have the skills to manage it anymore.
- It doesn't work for our business model anymore.
- Performance is very bad (could be latency, CPU horsepower, or memory, etc.).
- Maintenance cost is going up drastically.

Department-driven projects

- The current process is manual and relies too much on Excel spreadsheets or paper.
- The current process takes a lot of time.
- The current way takes lots of people.
- The current process is cumbersome and creates lots of errors.
- We are losing a lot of money with the current tools.
- We can quickly improve productivity by a certain percentage.
- We can easily grow revenue/profit by X percentage if we buy this.

While these can be very valid business justifications, unless data and sound facts support them, they are just opinions. The best thing you can do is to dig deeper to seek factual data and see if those claims are supported.

It is most likely there will never be real evidence of a direct correlation between the requested change and an increase in revenue, productivity, or profits. However, just because we cannot quantify the benefits and nail down all the specific details, should we reject the proposal? The answer is, not necessarily. That's why we need to have the second step where we check for alignment with the highest-level stakeholders.

For example, someone from the sales team is proposing a new CRM system and claims the potential exists for a 20 percent revenue increase. Although they may not be able to provide exact details of where that extra revenue is going to come from, you should be able to check with the VP of sales, the CFO, and/or the CEO for their opinion on whether such a system could indeed improve revenue. If they concur, then even if there is not a proven business case, you have proper alignment with high-level stakeholders for that decision.

Calculating total cost of ownership (TCO) is another critical aspect of the business justification process. Many times, capex proposals only outline the initial investment required for the project's first phase. Also, proposals often don't include other cost components needed to implement the project that would be paid for through operating budgets. You must understand that you are making a decision for all future phases and all project costs irrespective of whether they can be capitalized. Then, and then only, you can make a wise decision based on the business case and alignment for that level of investment.

Here are typical itemized costs you would want to see in any project proposals for all phases of the project:

- The initial purchase cost for all components—hardware, software, databases, middleware, operating systems, third-party products

- Implementation or setup services cost
- Configuration and integration costs
- Annual maintenance cost
- Internal labor cost for configuring/implementing a system
- Incremental IT and user department labor cost for managing the new system

Many times, users or applications teams driving major software purchases may not understand all the underlying hardware and infrastructure costs or assume that those will be taken care of by someone else, hence showing a partial TCO picture.

The key to your TCO model is that it must include all direct and indirect costs, for all phases of the project, and should be built for a period equivalent to the life of that asset. Sometimes, total project costs can go up three to four times when you add all the cost components for the system's lifespan. That's the real number that your business case must be evaluated for.

If you use these simple yet robust strategies for approving capital spending, you are likely to have well-controlled depreciation expenses over time. Moreover, you may even find depreciation going down over time because assets are fully depreciated once their accounting life is over. However, your asset's functional life is much longer than that, and you don't need to spend as much money again to re-implement such systems.

3. Hardware and software

If this isn't already the most significant expense category, it sure will be very soon for most IT shops. This expense category includes all operating expenses related to hardware, major hardware maintenance, software maintenance, and all cloud computing services. Since the Cloud is just a different business model, this also includes all cloud subscription costs.

Unlike the other two major categories we discussed earlier, labor and depreciation, this expense category is not as tangible because a sizable sum goes toward warranty premiums, i.e., maintenance support costs for hardware and software in case something goes wrong. So just like many warranty services, a huge gap exists between cost and value for this type of expense.

Because this is a biggest expense category, a huge potential exists for steep cost reductions in this area. Let's look at all the subcategories in detail, along with common pitfalls and the best actions you can take to reduce costs here, both short- and long-term.

3.1 Expensed hardware and software
Approximately 6-8 percent of total IT cost
Reduction potential: 1-3 percent of this category's total
Cost-Value quadrant: 2

This is another modest expense in IT budgets. While the unit costs in this category are small, by the time you factor in the volumes needed, the total annual cost can add up rather quickly.

This category includes low-cost, short-life hardware such as desktop computers, laptops, monitors, peripherals, printers, desk phones, or mobile phones, etc., and low-cost software like Microsoft Office.

In most companies, any hardware or software that does not meet the capitalization threshold or life cycle test fall into the expensed hardware/software category.

The most common pitfalls for this expense are:

- Either too stringent or nonexistent standards
- Poor/Nonexistent volume discounts
- Unnecessary purchases
- Unwise leasing instead of buying
- Insufficient refresh cycle policies
- Unnecessary warranties
- Unmonitored/Unanticipated technological shifts

Standards—If you are a global company with offices around the world, having stringent standards for such commodity hardware can backfire. Because all such hardware is procured locally, if a company defines a global standard that dictates specifications, make, and model but fails to get volume discounts in each locale, one can end up spending too much money. At the same time, having no standards is not a good idea either because then every location ends up buying something different.

Having the right standards is critical. For example, in case of laptops, you can define three different specifications (low, medium, high) for CPU, memory, graphics cards, and operating system version. Then you allow local offices to procure equipment with those specifications from local sources. The same is true for cell phones, printers, or peripherals. Having stringent standards that specify more than a few key parameters for all these categories often backfires.

These kinds of standard specifications work for desktops and laptops but may not work for other commodities such as desktop phones, which largely depend on your backend phone system. Desk phones are mostly one-time expenses (buying the phones) and are pretty much considered a commodity. There isn't much room to reduce costs in this category beyond finding the right fit and negotiating volume discounts. Depending upon the number of phones you manage, a small reduction in unit price can add up to a substantial sum.

Volume discounts—Because this kind of hardware is procured routinely, a few units at a time, you may not get the desired volume discount. Having a contractual agreement with a provider to build successive discounts based on total volume makes sense. When you cross the first threshold, you qualify for one level of discount; then you work toward the next level by purchasing more from that vendor, and the cycle goes on from there.

Unnecessary purchases—Usually, desktops and laptops come with a preloaded operating system (OS), but if you have an agreement with the OS provider, such as Microsoft, you would be paying Microsoft for that OS separately. In this instance, you may end up paying double for the OS on any given asset. Once again, while the unit cost may not be too much, it adds up quickly.

Leasing versus buying—We will discuss this topic in detail in the next chapter focusing on common underlying factors that drive up IT costs. However, in my experience, it is a fifty-fifty proposition whether leasing or buying makes more sense in this expense category. The simple rule is to calculate your total cost of ownership (TCO) for each unit over its lifespan, say three to five years, and compare leasing costs to buying. If leasing is no more than 15 to 20 percent more than outright buying, leasing is often a good choice because you can spread the cash outlay over three to five years. However, in some countries, I found that leasing costs can be as high as double or triple the total cost of the asset and, in that case, you are better off buying assets outright.

Refresh cycle policies—This is probably the most significant factor in the total cost of this expense. For all commodity hardware, such as laptops, desktops, cell phones, or peripherals, technology is changing so fast that you can get substantially better and/or faster models every twelve months. The key is to determine whether you really need the latest and greatest technology every year. In most cases, buying the newest model gadget does not create commensurate benefits in productivity.

Many companies have defined refresh/replacement cycles, often three years. There are some benefits to such defined refresh cycles, but you almost certainly end up paying more over time. If employee morale and excitement can add tangible benefits from such periodic refresh, then it may very well be worth doing a forced refresh. However, if you are cash-strapped, you are better off with a break-fix replacement policy. With a break-fix replacement policy, you do not have a defined life cycle for a given machine. You will replace it whenever it breaks, whether in two years or five.

Unnecessary warranties—If you have shopped for electronic gadgets, you have seen that sales representatives push to sell you warranties, which are appealing when you are buying something new. However, if you are buying it thousands of times every year, warranties will almost certainly end up costing a lot of money for something you will never use. I can't think of a reasonable scenario where buying these expensive extended warranties ever makes sense for such commodity items.

You are better off just keeping some units in your buffer inventory to replace faulty ones. The cost of buffer inventory is far less than the total cost of warranties on all the machines. Warranties are protection for the failure of hardware where the manufacturer will replace the part or repair the unit. If you have a warranty and need to send the machine to the manufacturer for repair/replacement, you will need to have some other unit in your buffer inventory to ensure that user can work while the manufacturer is repairing the device. In either case, with or without warranties, you would need buffer inventory to keep work flowing. Warranties, and the imaginary peace of mind they bring, don't help business operations at all, but they certainly can cost you a lot of real money.

Technological shifts—This is very important but often poorly capitalized upon. Although new types of personal computers come to market every year, most companies are still using desktops and/or laptops with the Windows operating system, which costs a lot of money. In addition to the cost of hardware, you also pay the provider for licensing their operating system.

However, with the advent of the internet and cloud computing, the demands on a personal computer today are much different than those of just five years ago. If you can do most of your work in the Cloud, then you are better off with Google Chromebooks or equivalent PCs at one fourth the cost of Windows PCs. If you are not entirely cloud computing enabled and need a full-fledged machine, the total cost of owning an Apple computer, which comes with the operating system installed, is less than the total cost of comparable Windows machines plus the cost of operating system.

If you are a 100 percent Windows operating system-based environment and can shift even 25 percent of your users to Chromebooks or Apple

MacBook, you will see significant reductions in your total cost over three to five years.

While cost alone may be a good enough reason for such a technological shift, it also has significant benefits in greatly enhanced security and durability. Either Apple MacBook or Chromebooks are far less susceptible to cyber risks than any leading Windows PCs. They also can last twice as long. When you combine total cost, life, and security benefits, it makes perfect sense for many corporations to change from a single standard Windows PC environment to a hybrid model.

3.2 Software maintenance
Approximately 10-15 percent of total IT cost
Reduction potential: 5-7 percent of this category's total
Cost-Value quadrant: 1

While the upfront cost of buying software is treated in most cases as a capital investment, these software purchases also have an undesired piggyback clause that tags on annual software maintenance as a percentage of the original purchase price or list price, which is much worse. This is a favorite revenue stream for software companies because it guarantees annual revenue in perpetuity without having to sell you additional software.

Payments for annual software maintenance is a significant chunk of money, typically consuming between 10 and 15 percent of IT spending. Unfortunately, it's also one of the low value-added costs. In many cases, it's a mandatory line item. But in other cases, it's considered necessary by internal staff simply out of habit.

Let's first understand what these maintenance fees are. They are paid every year to cover new product features (releases), software patches, and bug fixes. The annual fee is typically between 15 and 25 percent of the cost of the perpetual software license. The software support is typically limited to problems with their code, so they offer technical help if the software crashes or has bugs.

Technical support and new product releases are worth something, but not as much as what those cost. It's worth scrutinizing these costs at annual renewals. You may find that the most resistance comes from IT staff themselves. In many cases, they even forget it's optional.

Here are five questions you should ask before renewing maintenance agreements:

1. Are we contractually required to buy this maintenance contract?
2. How many new product releases have we used in the last two years? Do we really take advantage of new versions of this software?
3. How many times did we call technical support in the last year?
4. What will happen if we do not buy or renew this maintenance?
5. What's the right level of support for us? (Many software vendors have multi-tier support models at varying price points).

You may find that in many cases, you never used technical support at all, aren't using new product releases, and yet keep buying it every year just because you have always done so—or because of the high cost of restarting maintenance in the future.

Please note that eliminating maintenance contracts from all your software is not a good strategy either. The real challenge is building a good business case for either having or not having support, and if you choose support, identifying the right level and type.

That said, in general, if you can live without maintenance for three years and the system isn't mission-critical, you may be better off discontinuing it. Be ready to buy it again whenever you need to upgrade. Sales teams will be more motivated to sell you newer versions of their software at a good price when you're not on the hook with a maintenance contract. And your new price may even be less than what you would have spent over previous three years in maintenance fees.

If you cannot completely get off maintenance support, your second option is to explore third-party maintenance. Some outstanding companies and systems integrators provide much better support at a fraction of the cost. However, they cannot offer new features or product releases. You can save lot of money by just switching to a third-party maintenance provider and getting much better support.

After all the analysis is done, you have four choices for each maintenance renewal:

1. Keep it as-is (no change)
2. Lower the support tier level
3. Transition to third-party support
4. Terminate it altogether (most reduction)

If you use this approach with every renewal, you will find that many maintenance contracts can, indeed, be replaced by the other options listed above instead of continuing the status quo. As a result, at the end, you are likely to see a nice reduction in your total costs to the tune of 5 to 7 percent. This could be the most significant cost reduction you can accomplish without affecting business operations.

3.3 Hardware Maintenance
Approximately 5-7 percent of total IT cost
Reduction potential: 2-4 percent of this category's total
Cost-Value quadrant: 4

Compared to software maintenance, this category of expense is more reasonable in cost and also has more tangible value. This expense has three major components: 1) replacement of faulty hardware components, 2) firmware updates and security patches, and 3) technical support in case hardware is not functioning per design.

Typically, this expense ranges from 15 to 20 percent per year of the cost of initial purchase of hardware, and in most cases, one year of maintenance is included under the warranty that comes with the initial purchase.

However, most partners sell three- to five-year support contracts upfront, and customers have a choice to add that at a reasonable price. That approach allows customers to amortize the whole purchase, including service cost, over time and gives them peace of mind.

The same principles apply to this category as in software maintenance. This expense is also strictly optional beyond the first year. You will have to ask the following questions when a decision between buying or renewing hardware maintenance comes up:

1. What does this maintenance cover, and is it optional?
2. How stable has the hardware been over the last two years?
3. How many support calls have we made in the last year?
4. How many times have we called to get broken hardware fixed?
5. How fast does part replacement turnaround need to be?

If you are buying hardware maintenance on every single piece of hardware from desktops to mainframe servers and everything in between, you are doing something wrong. You want to determine carefully which equipment needs such maintenance and which doesn't. Most hardware supporting core business processes needs some backup plan, but hardware supporting non-critical business processes, development, QA systems, or low value-added applications can live without maintenance support. A good rule is to ensure you have excellent support for all hardware that supports mission-critical systems (applications).

The last question—how quickly do we need the vendor to respond with a replacement part in case of hardware failure?—is the most important question. In most cases, vendors assume that you need a replacement part in less than four hours, and therefore, they price their maintenance contracts accordingly. Unless you are dealing with a mission-critical system that would stop your business, you may be fine with next business day (NBD) delivery without serious risk to business continuity. This slight change in service level can reduce maintenance costs significantly. Luckily, most vendors do offer different levels of service at varying price points. You just need to select the one that suits your needs.

With a lot of hardware, you are better off keeping spares around instead of buying support. For example, desktops and laptops, small access layer network switches, desk phones, mobile phones, or wireless access points would fall into this category.

Unlike software maintenance, hardware support and part replacement have a nice, third-party ecosystem where you can easily find support at an affordable price, and in many cases, it is better than what's provided by the original equipment manufacturer (OEM). Switching to third-party maintenance providers can easily cut your annual maintenance expense on any given piece/type of hardware in half.

Many OEM vendors will increase the price of maintenance on older hardware often doubling or tripling the cost because older equipment is difficult to support. This steep increase is designed to motivate customers to buy new equipment.

We will discuss hardware replacement (refresh) cycles in another section, but know that you don't want to replace hardware just because increases in maintenance fees. If the hardware is otherwise stable, you can buy the warranty upfront for up to five years. If you still want to continue using that hardware beyond five years, especially if it's in good, stable condition, then you are better off finding a third-party maintenance option that will be cost-effective and better quality.

In essence, you have the following five options when it comes to hardware warranty renewal:

1. Renew as-is (no change in cost).
2. Lower the tier of service (bronze, silver, gold, platinum).
3. Reassess which hardware needs maintenance contacts.
4. Transition support contracts to third-party providers.
5. Terminate support altogether.

After going through your hardware warranty and maintenance expenses and applying one of the above five techniques, you are likely to drop maintenance contracts on a lot of your equipment. In the end, this could cut your hardware maintenance bill substantially.

3.4 Cloud subscriptions
Approximately 10-15 percent of total IT cost
Reduction potential: 2-4 percent of this category's total
Cost-Value quadrant: 3

Today, we have cloud options for everything from software to hardware infrastructure and everything in between like the database or middleware. They are referred to by different names such as software as a service (SaaS), infrastructure as a service (IaaS), platform as a service (PaaS), but one can consider all these segments as different flavors of IT as a service (ITaaS).

The Cloud is the second biggest innovation in the IT industry after the Internet, and it has the potential to turn the whole industry upside down. The Cloud is a metaphor for the business model in which, instead of customers buying and managing all IT assets, someone else owns and operates the infrastructure. These two factors—ownership and management of IT assets—changed how IT services are procured, managed, delivered, and consumed. The reason for the exponential growth in cloud computing has to do with the long list of benefits that come with it, both for customers and providers. The overall value proposition for cloud transformation can be summed up in the following ways:

- **Scale**—Because cloud providers are managing similar assets/services for hundreds or thousands of other customers, they tap into economies of scale and all the cost advantage and efficiencies that come with it.
- **Opex Vs. Capex**—Customers don't have to make huge, upfront capital investments. Instead, they "pay as they go."
- **Systems Administration/Upkeep**—Cloud providers take over the responsibility for keeping up the software and hard-

ware so customers don't have to employ personnel to keep up or continuously enhance the new features. This is indeed a very nice benefit that is often taken for granted.

- **Upgrades on the fly**—Except for complex enterprise resource planning (ERP) systems or back-office systems, gone are the days of expensive, long, and yet mostly non-value-added upgrades. Cloud software providers release and manage the updates themselves with a little help from customers for the necessary testing. Cloud hardware providers upgrade the hardware behind the scenes and do it very well, which is also for their own benefit.
- **Total cost of ownership (TCO)**—Because of the above benefits, cloud offerings help customers reduce TCO, including the cost of procurement, provisioning, implementing, and managing software or hardware over its lifespan.
- **Speed**—The total time it takes to provision and enable cloud software or hardware is tenfold less than the traditional way of doing things from procurement to go-live.

It's no surprise that this is the fastest-growing category of IT expense. At some point in the very near future, it will likely be the biggest category of spending for all IT shops. For small- and medium-size newer companies, the Cloud is the default for all their software and hardware and is already their most significant IT expense. For large, global companies with a complex IT footprint, this category is slowly growing.

Although combined in one big category, software and hardware clouds have different value propositions and levers for managing the costs.

While there are lots of benefits, don't assume the Cloud is always the most cost-effective option. The way cloud subscriptions are structured, they almost always cost customers more in the long run. Some cloud services could end up costing you three to five times more over the lifespan of that software or hardware.

Let's first understand generic differences between the Infrastructure (hardware) Cloud and the Software Cloud.

Infrastructure cloud providers, such as Amazon, Microsoft, and Google continue to invest billions of dollars in building world-class data centers. They also use specially designed hardware that allows them to manage such large-scale infrastructure with high efficiency and the lowest cost. These providers are now capable of handling your entire IT infrastructure, including servers, storage, backups, disaster recovery, operating system administration, middleware, and databases.

Given the fierce competition among cloud providers, the cost of infrastructure cloud offerings are continually falling and are now becoming cheaper than the cost of owning and managing your own hardware. The very fact of steadily declining prices creates a high degree of business value and little potential for cost-reduction opportunities. However, that's not the case for the Software Cloud.

The cloud software industry is much different from the Infrastructure Cloud. In this segment of the Cloud, it's mostly software companies offering their own software via Cloud subscription. Some software companies only offer cloud versions of software, such as SalesForce.com, SAP SuccessFactors, Concur, Workday, and many more. Most other traditional software companies have also started offering cloud options in addition to their traditional way of selling perpetual licenses and maintenance. The industry has realized the enormous potential of long-lasting cloud benefits, so it's no surprise that today nearly 100 percent of software providers have cloud offerings.

Unlike the Infrastructure Cloud, the Software Cloud is considered a specialty cloud because its offering is provided by the original software developers. Customers do not have an option to use any other cloud provider for using particular software. Because of this, the Software Cloud never experiences falling prices.

The Software Cloud, therefore, has much less cost-reduction potential compared to many other expense categories. The best way to manage subscription software costs is to use other levers such as volume, contract term, purchase timing, and bundling of more products/services. The big levers software companies use to their advantage are:

- **Contract term**—The period for which you are obligated to pay for the software. Most prefer at least three years whether you continue to use the software or not.
- **Unit price**—This is how all subscriptions are quoted. It's typically the price per user per month. When quoted in per user per month terms, the software unit price is meager, which leads to poor decision making as a buyer.
- **Volume**—Minimum number of licenses that you must buy. The bigger the volume, the higher the discount offered. This also leads to over and early buying.

Knowing that these are the levers software vendors have, you can use these to arrive at a good win-win agreement that helps you lower the overall cost. However, please note that the best time to manage cloud costs is when you are buying for the first time. Once you begin using the software, renewals have some potential for optimizing costs but not much. Here are the things to consider:

Build a TCO model for the entire lifespan of the software (ten years)— In many cases, software use will grow and last five or even ten years. It's wise to construct a TCO model to see whether it's still cost-effective over that period. You may find that TCO over five to ten years would lead you to spend three to five times more than what it would take to own and manage that software yourself if that's an option. Understanding this TCO number helps you in your negotiations.

Negotiate lower per unit cost—Don't overlook the small numbers of unit prices quoted in per user per month numbers. These numbers quickly add up if you have ten thousand users and expect to use the software for ten years. Negotiate a lower per unit cost to the best of your ability, including some reductions based on volume thresholds as you increase the number of users over time. Compare that software to your on-premises options or competition (if feasible) to lower the per unit cost.

Start small and grow as you use the software—The second biggest lever is the number of users you bring to the table. Software companies would incentivize you to buy licenses for the entire user population. This can be a significant disadvantage for big companies where deploying the software could take several months or quarters. This leaves licenses sitting on the shelf accumulating dust and costing you hefty monthly fees while you are working to extend the software to every corner of your user base. Defining the project rollout schedule and tying the purchase of subscription licenses to actual implementation is another key lever in managing overall costs.

Pick the shortest term possible—This is another variable that potentially can be disadvantageous to you if the term of the contract is too long. In most cases, software vendors won't allow less than a two-year term, but most will make a case for signing up for three or five years. In return, many software companies do offer lower per unit prices if you sign up for a longer term. The best way would be to negotiate a shorter term with a price lock for additional years should you choose to extend beyond the initial term. Another way to limit your exposure would be to negotiate at least one exit clause with or without any caveats, while you test the software during the initial contract term.

Ability to lower the number of licenses—As discussed, buying too many licenses too early is a big factor in raising cloud subscription costs. Many providers do not allow you to reduce the number of licenses during the term of the contract. This creates a considerable cost burden if your software adoption does not meet your original plans, either in the number of users or the timeline. You would be stuck with large numbers of unused licenses for the entire term. If possible, negotiate a way to adjust license quantities up or down at least once a year.

Skip the premium support—This can be big and least value-added cost, like with traditional software maintenance. In most cases, you do not need such service, since your cloud subscription includes standard support and upgrades to all future versions of the software. As a rule, buying this type of premier service is not a good strategy. If you really need some help, you can pay for specific help to straighten out whatever issues arise. Please know that, irrespective of which service model you go with, the software provider will ensure implementation goes well. It is in their best interest to ensure your success.

Here are some common pitfalls beyond the cost dynamics we discussed that you should be aware of when it comes to cloud subscription services. These factors can be important negotiating levers that you can use in addition to or instead of cost reductions.

The vendor's reputation—Anyone can write new software and host it on their server sitting in their garage and call themselves a cloud provider. You must understand the details of where your software is hosted and how it's managed, even though you don't own it and you are not responsible for it. Most reputable software companies have either built their own data centers or host their software in one of the leading cloud provider's data centers. If the vendor has several hundred reputable companies as customers, you can take that as meaning they are an acceptable risk. In addition, you should also validate all their operational processes for data management, backup, cybersecurity, privacy protection, disaster recovery systems, administration controls, physical security, etc. Such validation provides the necessary comfort for relying on the vendor for sensitive systems and data.

Cloud vs. co-location—These are two different business models. In both cases, your hardware or software is hosted in somebody else's data center. Cloud refers to a business model where you don't own software and/or hardware, and your instance of the given software/hardware is managed by pooling the infrastructure for similar assets for other customers in what is called a multi-tenant model. On the contrary, co-location is simply renting a small space in a data center where you own and manage your hardware and software. Co-location is used for entirely different reasons than cloud-based business solutions.

Data security—While security controls provided by reputable cloud providers far exceed the controls any individual companies can afford, your data is invariably exposed to a third party. If that is not acceptable to you for any reason, then the Cloud may not be a valid option for you. Be cautious of low-cost and/or startup vendors, as your data may not be managed with state of the art security, irrespective of the vendor.

Data protection—Most reputable vendors have excellent data backups and disaster recovery/business continuity infrastructure in place in case something goes wrong with their primary data center. Once again, many low-tier cloud providers can't afford and usually don't have sound disaster recovery (DR) or business continuity plans (BCP). However, they may not explicitly tell you so unless you ask for it. This is another reason why you should stick to reputable vendors.

Data ownership and transition—All software vendors contractually agree that customers own their own data and have the right to access that data at all the times. However, in most cases, it is very challenging for you to retrieve your data if you terminate the contract. This makes it very difficult for one to leave a given cloud vendor.

As you can see from the discussion above, cloud computing is mainstream today. Understanding the dynamics of this business model and the strategies you can use to effectively manage these costs will help you in the long run. More and more of your budget can then be transitioned to the cloud cost.

4. Telecommunications and networks
Approximately 10 percent of total IT cost
Reduction potential: 2-4 percent of this category's total
Cost-Value quadrant: 3

A long time ago, telecommunications and networks was the biggest expense category, since many IT departments started with the need to manage huge, in-house phone systems and trunk lines. Then, with the advent of the Internet and desktops and laptops becoming commonplace, network circuits became the catalyst for collaboration outside the company's four walls. Network circuits primarily owned by leading telephone companies became an expensive line item in most IT budgets.

In modern-day operations, these expenses include:

- Telephone lines
- Cell phones
- Internet circuits
- High-speed private network circuits, such as multiprotocol label switching (MPLS)

Telephone lines—As IP Telephony (Voice over IP, VoIP) has become prevalent in the last decade, the (previously much more costly) expense of trunk lines and long-distance calls continues to shrink. With VoIP, costs went down, and at the same time, the quality and reliability of calls went up substantially. Today, most companies have transitioned to VoIP for the most part. However, many companies still have at least some traditional phone lines. There aren't many options to reduce this cost since very few vendors offer these services. So, just pick the one that's available in your area.

Cell phones—This is another significant and rising expense. It has three major components:

1. Equipment cost (usually replaced every two years)
2. Cost of monthly plans
3. Usage charges, especially roaming charges

The mobile phone business model in the United States, where the cost of the equipment is included in the price of the monthly plan if customers commit to two-year contracts, has spoiled the users. They are used

to getting new cell phones every two years. This model is complemented by the pace of technology, which changes the game drastically every
two years. Leading-edge technology for cell phones two years ago is likely obsolete today.

Monthly plan charges are where the bulk of the money goes. While many
phone companies have comprehensive plans, when it comes to enterprise
accounts, they have much more complicated terms, such as minimum
monthly or annual fees, pooling of minutes, pooling rules for data use,
roaming charges, hotspots, and tethering. On top of that, most cell phone
bills are also rife with billing errors that are usually not in your favor.

Roaming charges for calls and data due to travel is the most unpredictable
cost for cell phones. And it's by far the most complicated part of the cell
phone bill, which is very difficult to comprehend in the first place. It's also
a variable charge, based on user need and travel, so it is more difficult to
predict and control.

The best thing to happen in trying to control roaming charges was the
advent of VoIP and easy-to-use tools such as Skype, Google Hangout,
WhatsApp, and WeChat. You don't need international lines to make calls
using these apps; all you need is internet access, which is also becoming
ubiquitous and cost-effective everywhere.

Internet circuits—This is a significant and rising expense for IT budgets.
It's probably the most mission-critical service for any IT department
because most companies can't function even for minutes without internet access.

The cost of internet circuits is dropping fast as more and more players
enter the market, but these costs add up. If your company has global operations, you will need to engage with internet service providers (ISPs) in
each country. You also typically need primary and secondary circuits in
case of an outage.

Private network circuits—These are like internet circuits and are usually provided by the same vendors, but these circuits are closed to public traffic. Such circuits are used to connect various locations spread across town, the region, country, or even the world. The best way to connect your geographical locations is to use private circuits in a wide area network (WAN). While there may not be many circuits of this type in your budget, each unit is very expensive and represents a significant part of your budget.

These circuit costs are also coming down by using standard internet circuits with an added layer of security for private collaboration. Many big companies still use MPLS (multi-protocol label switching) type circuits that are very expensive. The unit cost of these circuits in some countries can be very high. The good news is that technology obsolescence is equally active in this segment. Over the next few years, many of these expensive, high-speed circuits will be replaced with more cost-effective technology referred to as software defined wide area network (SDWAN).

For the above four components in this telecommunication/network expense category, the pitfalls are universal, and therefore, remedies for managing these costs better are also typical. Here are the common pitfalls for this expense category:

- Long-term contracts
- Complicated terms with lots of variables that trigger overage charges
- Billing errors

All these pitfalls favor service providers, not customers. Most telephone and network circuit providers require at least a three-year binding contract, but most of them try to push for as many as seven years. The other terms of their agreements are also usually very rigid, irrespective of issues and inconveniences, and it's almost impossible to exit a contract early.

Complicated contract terms are another, similar level of defense these companies use to protect their revenue. Telecom contracts are by far the biggest contracts in the sheer number of contract documents one has to sign.

Because of these complicated terms, these bills are rife with billing errors. The monthly bills for any of these services, even for a mid-size company, can easily be up to 100 pages long, and most IT departments don't have dedicated analysts to verify these bills, so errors go unnoticed, and that can cost companies a lot of money.

Your best cost-reduction opportunity is to better manage these three pitfalls, but these are very complicated issues. You certainly can try to do it yourself, but this is a complicated area where specialized skills can be instrumental. The problems in this industry are so significant that there is a vibrant new sub-industry called Telecom Expense Management (TEM); it's composed of individuals and teams who have mastered managing these contracts, monthly bills, and negotiations with providers.

Most of these TEM service providers extend their services on a contingency basis where they evaluate your contracts and monthly bills and suggest clear strategies for reducing these expenses. They will take a portion of the savings directly attributable to their services, usually a third of the savings. This works as a win-win for both sides because this type of expense management requires a lot of skills, automation, and patience. Because their pay depends on customers saving money, these TEM service providers not only identify optimization opportunities but also work directly with the respective service providers to make the changes necessary to realize the cost savings.

In this chapter, we covered a lot of ground. We discussed all the major components of IT budgets, including labor costs, depreciation costs, hardware and software costs, and telecommunications/network costs. By analyzing each cost category and what it includes and knowing the most common pitfalls and, most importantly, the levers you can use to optimize these costs, you should be able to optimize your costs.

As discussed, it takes time to see the shift in your IT budget since most of these strategies take one to three years to take effect. Don't expect quick results. However, all the changes we discussed here are structural in nature so their benefits will last longer without you having to take any new actions every year.

CHAPTER 13

What Drives IT Costs Higher?

The common underlying factors

In the previous chapter, we discussed strategies for managing each cost component in detail. As you may have realized, all those techniques are applied after the fact in a reactive mode to help optimize the existing cost structure. Now, let's take a preventive approach and understand the common underlying factors that drive up the IT costs in the first place. This should help us avoid getting in a tough situation to begin with.

The factors discussed below are generic but apply to all IT costs as they form the backbone of the mindset and behaviors common in all IT departments. These behaviors also collectively describe how IT spending decisions are made.

1. Fear/Risk-averse mindset

This is a significant contributing factor in all IT costs. The majority of IT spending is driven by fear, whether such fears come from internal management teams, vendors, your user base, or industry publications.

Internal fears—Unfortunately, many IT shops are considered overhead or utility functions, but they still provide mission-critical services. They, therefore, are cautious to avoid any trouble from c-suite executives or users who are usually more powerful than IT departments. The solution is to avoid displeasure from senior management or users by covering all risks to the fullest extent possible. This approach ends up costing a lot of money.

External fear—IT departments avoid getting into unpleasant situations by buying service contracts. As we have seen, most of the low-value-added spending in the areas of software and hardware maintenance is driven by the fear of something not working or the technology falling behind, irrespective of whether you truly need it or not. The same is true for many other expenses, such as hardware maintenance, warranties on expensed hardware, or redundancies in infrastructure.

2. Too much redundancy—layers and layers of it

The mindset discussed above also manifests as multiple layers of redundancy in all aspects of IT. The best way to explain this is by outlining a typical IT scenario. Here is how most systems are managed:

An application (software) is hosted on multiple servers for each layer of the stack—database, application, web server, and storage. For each layer, there is usually at least one pair or cluster of servers to distribute the load (load-balancing) or failover (high availability) in case of a hardware or software failure. Collectively, this is called a production environment, which comprises multiple servers, storage devices, databases, and other such components.

This production environment is then complemented by at least two similar setups called development and quality assurance (QA) environments. The QA environment is pretty much the same caliber as the production environment, while the development environment can be a little trimmed-down version of the production environment. This, in effect, doubles or even triples the number of servers and storage devices required.

Once this environment is established, these environments are backed up with multiple copies captured daily, weekly, monthly, and quarterly. Many are incremental backups, while others are full-copy backups. All these backups are either stored on tape or disks off site. However, at any given time, you may be holding as many as 100 or more snapshots of backups taken at different times. Some old backup copies are purged based on data retention policies as new copies are created. These backups require specialized hardware, software, and storage vaults. Not to mention, clusters of this backup software and hardware are highly available in case a failure occurs in the backup gear.

While backup gear provides data protection, it is hardly useful in a real disaster because that data needs to be restored in the same application on similar hardware and connected to users to restore the service. This entails duplicating the entire production environment with all its duplicity to another data center and replicating the data in real time in the unfortunate event of a disaster in the primary data center. You also need to install networking equipment to connect to that second data center. Additionally, all that networking gear and circuits are at least duplicated to manage the redundancy. All the redundancies are pretty much duplicated in the second data center.

The disaster recovery (DR) data center, which will come into effect only in case of a major disaster, can take a great deal of time to bring online. Sometimes, these secondary DR datacenters can be designed in high-availability fashion with real-time replication and failover, which complicates the environment and adds tremendous costs.

Looking at the behind-the-scenes details of an application that users access from one screen and assume it's just another computer somewhere could involve more than 100 servers, pieces of storage hardware, network devices and circuits, backup software, backup libraries, and tapes. All of this is required to cover the multitude of risks with multi-layer redundancies—production, QA, development, high availability, load balancing, backups, disaster recovery sites, and a real-time failover data center. Moreover, in each of these segments, each component has added redundancies in case of the failure of any one component.

While these prevalent practices and risks must be mitigated, often people are surprised by the number of redundancies put in place to ensure the continuity of business services (applications). Unfortunately, this over-redundancy is done irrespective of whether an application is mission-critical or a peripheral system used by a small group of users once a month.

Because this is done by the book and seen as a best practice, in a business context, this spending is rarely questioned.

These decisions are often made by back-end IT folks who are focused on ensuring continuity of service "at any cost," even if the aggregate cost is much higher than the business value the service generates. While these are all business risk decisions, most people outside of IT do not have the skills to understand the behind-the-scenes details. They, therefore, leave it to IT management, which, if driven by fear and risk aversion, will end up costing the company a lot of money. As you can see, all these decisions are business decisions, not technical decisions.

3. Oversizing—buying too much too early

Basically, just don't do this. The best strategy is to define a deployment schedule upfront and tie purchases to actual consumption as users come onboard. Even if it costs a little more upfront, you will see how cost effective and risk mitigating this approach is, especially if there are delays in deployment.

The same is the case with oversizing hardware. Many a server, operating system, or database license is sold based on the number of CPUs, or cores. When vendors or system integrators size hardware, they are as conservative as possible in their assumptions of load and performance. In such cases, you end up buying equipment that may be required three years from now, and by then, the original hardware is already outdated. Also, know that many major software implementations still take a year or so, and during that time, you don't need much beyond the development environment. Buying too big and too early ends up costing a lot of extra money.

4. Technology push vs. business pull

This is another factor possibly leading to excessive IT spending. We discussed this phenomenon from a value management perspective earlier.

If IT teams predominantly decide to get the latest and greatest technology, you end up spending a lot of money for the newest technology, which may or may not directly benefit the business.

The most common justification IT teams use for getting new technology is that the current technology (hardware or software) is old. Which, by itself, is not a good reason to buy the newest technology. Unless you are lacking some critical business features and it is preventing you from achieving business goals, you may want to wait until you actually need to update your technology. New technology can be, and often is, good, but it may cost much more than the business value it can potentially provide.

Having said that, a technology push aligned with business goals is good for the company. CIOs who make connections between business problems and technological solutions provide the perfect opportunity for business-driven technology push.

5. IT procurement decision makers

Who should make the decisions for IT procurement involves very important dynamics primarily driven by whether the CIO is business-minded or a technical expert and who is the final authority in spending decisions. In most companies, the ultimate decision makers on big-ticket items are CEOs or CFOs. While they are, indeed, experts in strategic and financial decisions and ensuring spending supports business goals, they are least equipped with technological decision making. Very few CEOs and CFOs understand the rationale behind many technical investments, especially hardware. They can relate, to some extent, with the software side's benefits, but that also has many technology aspects they don't understand.

The people (or person) influencing CEOs and CFOs in such technical decisions make a big difference. If CIOs are purely technical experts, they wouldn't understand the connection between technical and financial decisions and business results.

An ideal scenario would be having a business-driven CIO who understands both sides of the coin, technical and business—someone who is trusted by both IT professionals and other stakeholders. Someone who can understand the strategic value of technology and plot a course toward the best solution for the company.

6. Disconnect between IT and the company's mission

This disconnect is a similar phenomenon to the technology push versus business pull conflict we discussed earlier. In most traditional companies, IT teams perform the utility function of keeping current systems running. They are not at the forefront of business decisions. They are considered a necessary overhead expense and sometimes report to someone who is far removed from the business' epicenter. However, this phenomenon is rapidly changing as more and more CEOs realize information technology's potential effect on success or failure. With this realization, many progressive companies are bringing their IT teams to the forefront.

In traditional companies where IT is a utility function, IT managers struggle to make a connection between their decisions and the company's mission. This, unfortunately, leads to many misaligned spending decisions.

For example, your company could be fighting for survival due to massive debt, interest payments, and falling revenues, and your spending decisions should be frugal. However, IT managers unaware of those dynamics could keep pushing technology spending to ensure reliability, stability, and/or performance. If you have IT manager who understand technical choices but don't connect to business goals, you almost always end up with unwise spending.

Conversely, another example would be a struggling company that could benefit by improving its sales team's effectiveness with some IT investment. However, if all the IT spending is instead directed toward expensive technical upgrades that do not directly add revenue, there isn't money left for buying sales tools. Here you have a missed opportunity due to misalignment.

This gap may not be evident to most people outside of IT, but unfortunately, about two thirds of IT spending goes directly toward keeping the current technology running, not innovating or growing the business. Most of that money is taken up by expensive technical spending that could be easily optimized.

7. Not understanding sales processes

Buying IT technologies is a specialized skill. Buying IT products and services is difficult not only because of technology's complex nature but also because you are working with highly trained sales professionals. IT folks, on the other hand, are not trained properly in the procurement processes.

IT pricing is value-based pricing, not cost-plus markup-based pricing. The value is very subjective and different from one customer to another. Value is also based on how badly you need that product and the extent of benefit you could get from it. Based on those two factors, one may pay a considerable sum while others may pay less.

Because different people in the same company value products differently and at a different stage in the purchasing cycle, IT vendors prefer to connect with the people in functional organizations who will value their products or services better. Purchasing or IT departments are likely to value certain products less than what the end user or business process owner would.

CIOs need to be aware of this overall dynamic so they can work effectively with all the stakeholders and vendors. CIOs should also invest in getting all their managers trained in the IT procurement process.

8. Software audits

Unlike hardware, the software can be copied or installed on many more machines than what you are entitled to. The only control on software use is through contracts. Most users or IT team members are several steps removed from the contract terms and may not even be aware of their actions that could breach the contracts.

Because software could be used by more people than you are entitled to, most contracts include broad audit rights by the software vendor. Software vendors often request and perform such audits. Any discrepancies they find result in a penalty that must be paid. However, it's born out of the customers' improper use of the software in the first place.

Because software use rights are defined only in contracts, there is room for a lot of creativity in defining those rights. Most of the time, customers don't put enough thought into understanding whether those rights can be effectively managed and controlled in real life. Below are some examples of the metrics by which software could be sold. For each of these metrics, the actual definition could vary from one software vendor to another.

- Named user
- User
- Concurrent users
- Active user
- Passive user
- Light, medium, or heavy user
- Named employee
- Records in database
- Legal entity
- Physical location
- Country
- Revenue
- Enterprise
- CPUs
- Cores

- Hardware serial numbers
- Number of transactions per quarter/year

What complicates matters more is that the same software may have multiple components, and each of those components can have different metrics. Also, there could be numerous cascading metrics. For example, you could be licensed for certain transactions volume in a year but also have an additional threshold for specific type transactions (subset) not exceeding a specified threshold in a month or year. These are designed very restrictively and are not difficult to trip over inadvertently.

What's bad about cost overruns driven by software audits is that they are unplanned increases. Payments for overuse based on audit findings usually come from funds earmarked for much more valuable items.

So what can you do about it? First, ensure that you understand all the contract terms you must abide by. Second, do everything possible to ensure you are 100 percent compliant at all times. You should put most of your energy on the preventive side to avoid getting into these situations. Establish a sound IT asset-management process that validates current usage against entitlement periodically to ensure full and continuous compliance, including, but not limited to, contracts control, controls for adding or terminating users promptly, and quarterly contract review for major thresholds. Having such a methodical process also helps to demonstrate to vendors that your company values software usage rights and any discrepancies are more likely driven by complexity of the software and/or contract terms. Conversations in such scenarios are a lot more productive for both parties and usually end up in a win-win situation.

On the other hand, you also need to be well prepared for audits when they occur by having a well-established procedure for handling audits. The more defined your process, the more effective it will prove.

Here are some guidelines you can establish for managing your software audit process:

- Establish a single point of contact globally, preferably in the legal department, who is responsible for handling any compliance claims.
- Define a checklist of procedures that must be followed within your company that you can send to the auditor.
- Ensure you have a multi-party non-disclosure agreement (NDA) in place. Often, there is a contract but no NDA between the customer and software vendor. There is hardly ever an NDA between the customer and a third-party auditor. Insist on three-party NDAs based on your legal department's template.
- Review the claim carefully and find any errors or apparent omissions. It happens more often than you think.
- Ask for a copy of the latest contract the vendor has on file against whatever they are auditing. Usually, there are multiple contracts and amendments over time, and you want to make sure the vendor is keeping their records clean as well.
- If there is an actual claim in the initial audit notice itself, ask for the evidence and how they gathered it. Some software has hidden code that sends alerts to the software vendor, and some vendors just come in and check software use themselves without going through you. Such actions are only okay (legal) if stipulated in your contract. If software vendors do not follow the rules, you want to be aware of it. If they are unable to provide evidence, you can push back on the audit claim.
- If everything is in order, provide acknowledgment and lay the ground rules for the audit. Simple ground rules would stipulate that auditors work only with a designated representative and should contact no one else, without exception. You must be in full control of the process.
- Another natural action you should take is to halt any new business discussions while an audit is in process. This procurement block is very effective and makes sense because you do not want to create new compliance-related issues until the current claim is resolved.

- During the actual audit, pay attention to every detail. Many times, vendors want to run their scripts to determine use. See if they are contractually allowed to do so. If they are indeed allowed, use your change-management procedures and calendar to perform such tasks so they don't affect your business operation.
- Once evidence is collected, the vendor should provide you with a detailed statement of your allowed versus actual use. Verify all the details in their report. Do not assume everything they present is correct and without error.
- Once you agree there is discrepancy, you will have to pay for the overuse. Most software vendors would provide you various options to rectify the situation, including buying additional licenses, buying other products, swapping some licenses from an unused category, or committing to a larger/longer business relationship. You can use any of these or even propose your own options to negotiate a win-win agreement that resolves the situation.
- Realize that, while software vendors want to be rightfully paid for overuse, they are ultimately interested in ensuring your long-term business. They wouldn't want to cut off the relationship abruptly. Use your long-term commitment as leverage in your settlement negotiations.

9. Long-term contracts

Contracts govern most IT spending, and very few contracts are for less than one year. While the most common term of any contract is three years, some can extend to five or even seven years. Longer contract terms usually give you excellent protection against cost increases and other favorable terms, but that can also end up being a cause of some excess costs.

Many times, your needs change during a contract's term, but if you are locked into a term, it's challenging to change the cost structure. For example, most software cloud services contracts are based on named user count, and if your user count never reaches the threshold you bought or goes down from current levels, you would continue to pay for the higher numbers through the end of your term.

Another example, your contract for helpdesk or data center operations monitoring may be for five years. There are lots of caveats on service level agreements, headcount used in delivering services, hours anticipated, and such. There are also a lot of overrun clauses where providers can charge you more money for crossing those thresholds. Overall, those costs can be burdensome, and you may want to explore other options.

If you are locked into a complicated, long-term contract, there is very little you can do about it. However, you can reengage with the service provider and improve the aspects of the contract that may be negatively impacting you. In most cases, service providers are willing to change some terms in the best long-term interests of both parties. We discussed "renegotiating the terms" as a good choice for some of the high-cost, high-value-added services in the earlier sections.

The purpose of discussing all these underlying cost factors is first to recognize their existence. That knowledge then helps you better address the cost overruns that stem from these factors. Also, note that not all the underlying cost factors discussed above may relate to every company. Some factors may be more relevant to your situation than the others. The strategies we discussed in the previous chapter, both generic cost-optimization strategies and specific tactics for each category can help you overcome the effects of these above factors.

CHAPTER 14

Common Myths about IT Cost Savings

Now that you understand all the cost factors and associated pitfalls, it may be a good idea to discuss the most common myths around IT cost management. As a CIO, you will get a lot of advice from your peers, superiors, executive team members, and even board members about different cost-management strategies. They have either heard of or read about such strategies or have had personal experience themselves. Sure, most strategies are sound, but you will find that one approach may well succeed in one company but fail miserably in another.

The key to understanding these strategies is to understand that there is a great deal of a gray area involved in each, and that gray area can make the difference between success and failure. Knowing common caveats in these strategies can help one understand whether a particular approach will succeed or fail in your situation.

I have tried all strategies in one form or the other. I have seen successes as well as failures using the same approach in different companies. This uncertainty is because these strategies are simple on the surface but have plenty of variables underneath. Here are the most common IT cost-savings myths.

IT costs are based on revenue

The most common metric of IT cost used is measuring total IT spending as a percentage of revenue. In many ways, this is the most harmful metric from an IT executive's perspective. However, as the most common metric, you have to use it whether you like it or not.

A lot of misconception exists about this metric. What it implies is that all IT costs are directly correlated to company revenue. Alternatively, in business accounting terms, all IT costs are variable costs. As such, if revenue increases, IT costs could go up, but as revenue drops, IT costs should go down. Nothing can be further from the truth. In reality, no IT costs are variable. One-hundred percent of IT cost are fixed costs

Economies of scale is another factor—one should expect to see lower IT cost as a percent of revenue as revenue increases, but this is driven by economies of scale and is not based on the unit cost of the product you sell. In other words, as revenue goes up, the IT costs may not increase in the same proportion. Most of the IT infrastructure can scale up at much lower costs than what's needed for the initial purchase. For example, if your revenue doubles, your total IT team headcount may not necessarily double in size. It may grow only a little based on whatever may be changed in the IT landscape.

Another critical factor is the scope of IT services. As we have seen, no two IT departments cover the same breadth or depth of services. The broader and deeper the services portfolio you serve, the higher the cost to deliver it. One can provide IT services at whatever threshold one wants based on cost as a percentage of revenue, but you may not get the same breadth of IT services.

This metric, therefore, does not serve as a good gauge for whether your IT department costs are competitive compared to those of your peers. However, it does serve one vital purpose. I use this metric to gauge the company's IT budget and how much we can afford, but not for how much IT costs. From that perspective, the IT budget is based on a robust metric that ensures we are not spending outlandishly on IT compared to other costs that are measured as a percent of revenue. This helps us to spend within the company's means.

Outsourcing your IT can reduce the cost significantly

Outsourcing may or may not reduce your costs. This is another phenomenon that no IT departments can escape addressing. Lots of good reasons exist for outsourcing, but cost savings is not near the top on that list. However, many times, this option is thrown in the mix to cut costs, which it can do, but only in the right circumstances. Many documented cases reflect that outsourcing has cost companies more money, both in direct and indirect costs. We are, therefore, seeing many companies reversing their course, at least on some outsourcing components.

Outsourcing is a broader term and has different forms. In some cases, companies prefer to stop doing certain tasks and instead get them done by external providers that specialize in such tasks. In other cases, they may use contract labor instead of employees due to a variety of reasons.

If one is considering totally outsourcing IT under the premise of cost savings, it's guaranteed to fail. It's only an option for small retail shops or small family businesses, but for any sizable corporation, it's a non-starter.

If you are a global business and already have a presence in other countries, your overall current costs are likely much lower than any outsourcing provider. Again, you might still do the outsourcing for other good reasons but not for the cost savings.

The key is to focus on the reasons for outsourcing, such as lack of internal skills, temporary surge capacity, or expertise in new advanced technology and then do selective, piecemeal outsourcing. In some cases, it may appear to save costs on the surface, but it may not be enough to compensate for additional costs arising from this shift. Outsourcing comes with its own challenges and additional costs, such as time lapse, communication gaps, poor quality, rework, the effectiveness of individuals far removed from the business, and so on. Evaluate the purpose of your outsourcing. If it's solely driven by cost savings, then pause and do a full cost-benefit analysis before taking the next steps.

Cloud transition can cut cost significantly

I get a common question these days: "Why don't we scrap the data center on our premises, go to the Cloud, and reduce the cost?" That, indeed, is an option and may reduce the total cost of ownership for many IT services. However, for any sizable global company, not everything can be or should be taken to the Cloud, at least in the current state of the Cloud's maturity.

The Cloud is, indeed, a wise strategy for select applications and services. For example, most companies are scrapping their local email servers (MS Exchange or Lotus Notes) and successfully transitioning to one of the Cloud's email platforms. The total cost of ownership in such transitions is much lower in the Cloud than for an on-premise solution. It's true for many other applications as well. Moreover, luckily, more and more applications are being enabled in the Cloud successfully. Cloud adoption will go up significantly over the next few years and decades.

However, there are many other IT services for which transitioning to the Cloud may not save any cost and can also deteriorate the quality of service. For example, if you have developed custom applications that are core to your business, those must be fully managed by your own IT resources. A cloud provider, at best, can rent you hardware and house those servers in their data centers. In such cases, the cost savings of hosting a few servers in the Cloud or colocation data center is likely to be much higher than adding those to your on-premise data center, especially if you have a data center for other applications already.

Another example would be mission-critical and data-intensive applications in manufacturing where any interruption in service could cost you dearly. Your cloud services are only as good as the quality of your internet or cloud circuits. If those are not reliable, your users can't get to those cloud applications from time to time and lose precious time.

Having said that, going to the Cloud is an integral part of IT strategy, and most companies will go in that direction for many reasons, but cost savings is likely to be at the bottom of that list. You shouldn't shy away from the Cloud, but use it wisely and where it makes sense.

Leasing or subscription models are cheaper than capital expenditures

Leasing versus buying is another misunderstood phenomenon. A small amount based on subscription or leasing cost per month, per unit is much easier to digest than a quote with significant numbers attached to a multi-year contract. We discussed this in the cloud subscription pitfalls section.

In more than 95 percent of the cases, leasing or subscriptions have substantially higher total cost of ownership (TCO) over the life of an asset compared to buying the asset outright as a capital expenditure. The leasing option is viable in a cash flow crunch, but it comes with a substantially higher TCO because it includes the cost of capital plus risk contingencies on your credit worthiness.

Another argument for leasing is that we get to replace the asset after it gets old and we will get some residual value versus throwing away that old asset. While this is true on the surface, the residual gain is often so low that it's not worth factoring into the cost evaluation.

The best strategy is to build your total cost of ownership (TCO) model for the life of that asset and determine which option is economical. Even if the TCO in leasing option is slightly higher, say by 10 to 15 percent, it is a good option to go with. If leasing is pursued due to a cash flow crunch, then it makes perfect sense to lease, irrespective of TCO in the other scenario.

Health checks or value engineering exercises can help reduce costs

Vendor-sponsored software health checks are another myth that should be qualified appropriately. Most of the time, health checks are pitched as risk-free and cost-free. I would argue against both. They are neither cost-free nor risk-free.

First, although there is no direct cost, most of your energy goes into educating vendors on your current IT landscape before they can provide their recommendations. Health checks cost companies a lot of money in indirect costs.

Secondly, most of these health checks are rife with risks. Exercises like these uncover license compliance issues. I would in no way encourage any companies to be noncompliant nor hide anything from vendors. However, as we discussed in the software audit section earlier, compliance adherence activity should be an integral part of your IT operations and asset management such that you never get out of compliance. You do not want to mix these two efforts at any point.

As a rule, such health checks exercises should not be done with the intent of cost savings. The right reasons to do such health checks would be to validate whether the current system is functioning as designed or if you have specific pain points. Such purposes are well served when health checks are done by independent, third-party system integrators who may already be familiar with your environment. You don't have to spend any energy to educate them on your current environment. They are in a much better position to provide you an unbiased view of gaps and opportunities to address them to improve the overall health of your system environment.

All the phenomena discussed in this chapter are viable actions that all IT departments will pursue from time to time. The purpose of this section was to illustrate that even though many strategies discussed here are pitched for the cost-savings reason, usually the real benefits are not the cost savings but other equally tangible benefits. CIOs should be aware of that and pursue these strategies in broader context than just cost savings. For example, cloud transition will have benefits in system reliability and availability, but they may actually cost more. Same thing with outsourcing; when you add all the real and opportunity costs, you may realize it's not a viable option. In a nutshell, these strategies are fine; you just need to evaluate them in a much broader context than cost savings alone.

Although less important than business value and risk-management aspects, this whole discussion about cost management is an integral part of the balancing act CIOs must perform.

Part V

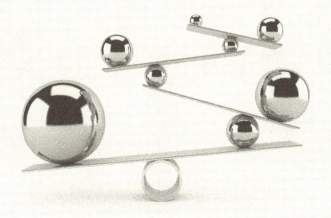

What Does It Take to Deliver the
"Perfect Imbalance"?

CHAPTER 15

Essential CIO skills

In the preceding three sections, we discussed the three major components of the CIO's role: value, risk, and cost management. That articulates very well the scope and expectations of the CIO position. However, just understanding those components, their interrelationship, and the way to achieve that perfect imbalance is not enough. What's most critical is to understand what it takes to deliver that perfect imbalance. This last section is dedicated to bringing all these factors together and understanding the essential skills of a CIO.

This book is not about leadership skills coaching, nor is it about human resource development. Most CIOs have had a fair amount of both formal and informal leadership development training. All of that training is essential and helps one improve their skills over time. However, most of that training is broad and not specific to the CIO as a technology leader.

Through my personal experience and conversations with other CIOs, below is a list of the most common and essential traits of successful CIOs. This list is by no means exhaustive, but you can count on these traits to contribute to your success. The below list of essential skills is not necessarily in any particular order. They all are equally important, but some are more integral to success than others.

Think like a CEO

One of my greatest mentors once gave me this gem, "Think like a CEO, not a CIO." That one piece of advice has had a profound influence over my career—it changed my whole attitude as a CIO. It pretty much flipped around my thought process overnight. To this day, no day passes where I don't come across a situation that reminds me of this thinking and I use it to correct my decisions and actions almost instantaneously.

Like many CIOs, if you have risen from the ranks, you have already proven your abilities and excelled in your technical and execution capabilities. Most likely, that's what made you successful and qualified for consideration for such a position. However, that background as a follower may not work well as a leader. Every time there is a new project or task, your mind gets into execution or the technical aspects of the situation to understand how big, challenging, and/or complicated such a project is. All the bad things flash through your mind about your team's skills, workload, cost pressure, competing priorities, risks, user perception, and so on. You then start articulating everything negative about this new project or task and not take a minute to think about why such a request came to you in the first place. In that mode, you fail to understand how the new project benefits the company as a whole. You then tend to think in your own world only when trying to understand the good or bad about it. However, IT is just one of the dozens of departments in the whole company, and your world is much smaller than the big picture of a company.

Thinking like a CEO is precisely the one trait that transcends all actions and decisions, whether they are technical, personnel, budget, prioritization, execution, or project deadlines. Every time you make a decision or give a subordinate direction, ask yourselves one question: Would this idea make sense if I were CEO? Most importantly, this changes the whole attitude of IT leaders, and they start thinking of themselves as part of a much bigger team that goes well beyond IT.

What exactly happens when you start thinking like a CEO instead of a CIO? This thinking allows you to look at everything that comes across your desk through the lens of a CEO who is responsible for every aspect of the company, not just one (IT). You would be surprised how remarkably different your decisions and attitude will be when you start looking at everything in the same framework as your CEO would.

Suddenly, you start thinking about revenue, profit, market share, productivity, customer satisfaction, quality, long-term viability, and so on in every decision instead of technical difficulties, risks, workload stress, team pressure, or similar risks.

Let me walk you through a simple example. Every company goes through ups and downs and must make some tough decisions from time to time. At some point in your career, you, as a CIO and a member of the executive team, may participate in a decision to downsize the company workforce. As the CEO and CFO suggest targets and overall parameters, you will have to make tough decisions about the best way to downsize.

If you approached that problem as a CIO, you would come up with lots of issues with downsizing and articulate the projects, workload, technical risks, turnover, morale and other problems. You would probably work very hard to make an argument that, because IT is so stressed, IT should not be downsized. You would be worried about how to deliver all the projects you signed up for with fewer people. That's your CIO thinking. There is nothing wrong with you because at the end of the day, you will be asked to deliver those projects.

However, if you stop for a minute to think like a CEO and understand what's driving this tough action and what's at stake for the company, you start thinking much differently. You are likely to scrutinize projects from a business value perspective and sift through which ones are critical for near-term business success versus which ones are not. You would even begin to think through which may be less value-added projects that you can push out. In the end, you would come up with an approach for correctly downsizing that best protects the company and IT goals and priorities.

The first approach, thinking just as a CIO, is obstructive and narrow, while the latter approach opens your thinking wide and is complementary and supportive. That's the day and night difference.

The above is just one example. You can run through this same thinking in every type of decision, whether related to hiring, buying, promoting, prioritizing, or developing a roadmap. Use this thinking like a permanent framework for your every action and you will be amazed by how gratifying the results are. If you must master only one of the many behaviors we discuss in this book, I would suggest focusing on this one. If you keep this one on all the time, you will never go wrong.

Have a clear vision

By "clear vision," we are not talking about you being a revolutionary or exceptional visionary. However, we are talking about your ability to strategize and develop a clear and strategic vision for where you want to be in three to five years. What's needed is your ability to grasp the current reality and create a horizon end vision for IT. It would help if you were able to define the destination and paint it in all its details for stakeholders. If you are unable to paint a picture of that end goal, you will have a hard time directing teams along the way. No one would know for sure what their destination is. Creating an end vision is not only needed for leading teams but also for aligning peers and departments so they can relate that end vision to the benefits.

Having a vision and plan is also an essential ingredient in creating excitement among subordinates. Your excitement fuels theirs and drives the pace of accomplishments because everyone is anxious to get to the destination. If the goal isn't clearly defined, then your speed will be very slow because your team has nowhere specific to go.

Creating a vision is not easy, and many CIOs fail in this crucial test. It requires an understanding of the state of technology, technical and business skills, maturity, and a clear understanding of business goals. Assessing the current state is easy, but precisely determining what's required to succeed is very difficult. It will be apparent only when you understand your company's mission over three, five, and/or ten years. If you don't understand the company mission, you will never be able to define a technology vision to accomplish that mission.

Every CIO's three- or five-year vision is specific to their company's mission and current state. For example, a few years ago, the CIO of a very well-respected, big technology company shared an essential element of his five-year vision to enable a single global instance of their ERP system. Now that seems like a trivial or irrelevant goal for many companies, and it is something most companies and CIOs take for granted because they accomplished this goal decades ago. However, this company is a very big conglomerate that grew exponentially in all regions, both organically and inorganically. In the process, they developed over twenty instances of major ERP systems for various locations. They spend a lot of money and time simply ensuring integration among all the ERP instances. By going to a single, global ERP, this CIO anticipated reducing substantial IT costs annually and recognizing hundreds of millions of dollars in intangible savings with anticipated efficiencies among all the business functions. Given the complexity of their business, five years is not a long time to accomplish such a monumental task.

The critical element of any vision is that it needs to be very simple and easy to articulate in one or two sentences. I have seen many presentations where the vision description takes a full paragraph and the mission statement takes two paragraphs. That kind of vision and mission doesn't go anywhere. You must create a picture of your endgame that is so simple to understand that everyone gets it without having to ask follow-up questions. They should only have follow-up questions on how to get there.

The more straightforward the vision, the easier it is to communicate, get support, and rally the troops behind it. If it is complicated, you will spend a few months merely explaining your end vision. The most powerful vision or endgame descriptions I found were often one or two sentences long.

Think business and act technology

If you master the skill of thinking like a CEO, this perspective will come naturally to you. The key is to always think business and act technology. In other words, translate business needs into technology requirements and, conversely, always ensure that technology is driving business results. Many times, CIOs forget the fundamental reasons IT even exists—to accomplish the overall business goals, tactical and strategic, of their organization. Your role in that business mission is to take care of the technology necessary to accomplish whatever the business' mission is.

CIOs make very few purely technical decisions. Even the most complicated technology decisions are a lot more about business than about the technology involved, so your every decision and action must be guided by the business' mission and not technology in isolation.

For example, you are evaluating a proposal to upgrade current technology with a newer and better solution. There may be healthy benefits with upgrade, such as better performance, enhanced speed, load reduction, greater reliability, and so on. However, if none of those parameters are currently a problem for your operations, there is no business benefit whatsoever. That value proposition, while it could be very potent for some other company, has no value to your business at this time.

Once you align your framework to think in business terms only, then all technology decisions are straightforward. Adopting that framework allows you to clear your mind of all the noise generated from such discussions.

Many of my subordinates are familiar with the types of questions I ask when they present proposals. What exactly is the business problem at hand and how will this solution help us achieve our business goals, like increasing revenue, profit, market share, quality, productivity, or service? How does it help us become efficient? How does it improve our customer's experience? And so on.

If the answers to these questions aren't as straightforward as these questions are, then you get a long, winding rationalization connecting the dots to make a remote business case. There are, indeed, many technology decisions that directly complement business objectives; however, many have little to no connection.

In a way, CIOs must continually work hard to ensure that their framework and mindset is tightly aligned with the business' goals. Technical goals should complement business goals. Technology is a means to achieving business objectives, not the end goal.

Act as a leader and don't seek oversight help

Leadership is another essential skill that CIOs must exhibit. CIOs are the heads of IT departments. They are the highest-level executive in charge of Information Technology. If you are in that role, don't expect any oversight from the CEO or others on your every decision. You must understand the business, the CEO's framework for decision making, your company's culture and financial position, and all other parameters of decision making, and then craft your team's actions to complement that. You must show the leadership your team needs.

That is not to say you won't have guidance to ensure perpetual alignment. However, usually you must translate what's not spoken or clearly articulated into an action plan for your team to support that business mission.

Not having oversight from the CEO or others is a blessing CIOs enjoy. Because, when a need for oversight arises, usually there is a problem with the CIO's credibility. Let's not confuse guidance, alignment, and feedback with oversight. Oversight is prescriptive and requires specific actions, versus guidance, which facilitates the meeting of minds. The CEO hired you to complement their mission with the technology you oversee, but they are not able to translate that for you. You must do that task yourselves.

Prove your technical expertise, a crucial prerequisite

A business mindset and leadership skills are essential, but technical expertise is critical. If you are not technically competent, nothing else matters. You are likely to do more damage than good.

I have seen several cases where CIOs came from other operational areas where they delivered exceptional results. In part, this happens with trusted leaders because they have demonstrated versatility in delivering results in many other areas. However, many such leaders don't succeed in IT because IT leadership requires a lot of technical knowledge. CIOs must understand technology enough to evaluate it within a business context. If you don't understand the technology, you are not able to translate business goals into technology speak. In the end, you would end up spending a lot of money and getting sub-standard results.

In such instances, you will see that the technology vision and roadmap may be aligned with business goals in concept, but in reality, they are far apart. You would also tend to see substantial cost increases in IT, partly because non-technical IT leaders are unable to question the proposals put forward by technical experts under them. When it comes to IT technology decisions, CIOs must understand both the technical and business sides of those decisions entirely and must be held accountable for making the right choices.

Capitalize on your credibility and trust

Trust from senior leaders, peers, and your team is essential for your success. You gain their confidence from your leadership track record, both in creating and executing the vision.

If you are new to the organization, your priority is to establish your credibility, which will translate into trust. You build credibility the hard way—by delivering real results. What got you in the door is your previous track record and all the conversations before getting the job. However, that must be translated into credibility by showing results.

Credibility is not only important among peers and superiors; it is also needed among your subordinates. They have to be able to trust you as a leader. They do that only when they see your credibility firsthand.

Your first opportunity for building credibility comes from assessing the overall situation and then quickly developing a comprehensive vision and IT roadmap. Once established, you must be able to sell your vision to all stakeholders. Your first test is going to be whether you grasped the problems correctly and have devised the roadmap priorities precisely. If you can succeed in this first step, you will have earned a token of credibility that allows you to go to the next level—getting the money, resources, and support to execute your plan. Then, as you deliver solutions in small phases, you continue to earn more credibility tokens.

The final test of your credibility is not executing IT projects and delivering technical solutions. The real and biggest test of your credibility is whether or not the company derives real benefits from the investment. If IT solutions don't deliver the promised results, your credibility—all you have earned to this point—is pretty much gone. However, if technical investments translate into the results you envisioned, your credibility can jump tenfold.

There are additional, equally critical aspects to ensuring your credibility. These include maintaining your peers' trust through partnerships. You earn credibility and trust from peers when you demonstrate you understand their needs, translate them into technical solutions, and deliver those solutions.

In the same way, your credibility as a leader also comes from the actual work you delivered with your team's help. Along the way, soft skills are vital. Your ability to treat people with respect, understand their views, mentor them professionally, remove roadblocks, and help them gain trust among users will earn their trust and respect, which is the foundation of credibility.

Recognize that *you* are the technology *leader* among your peers

There are two key aspects of technology leadership that CIOs must understand. The first is that the CIO is the only one qualified to make technical IT decisions and lead IT teams. The company depends on you to help make the right choices on information technology. Most of your peers or superiors are not equipped to make sound IT decisions. If others are making IT decisions and you are just executing their decisions, then you are not doing your job.

It's your responsibility to understand business needs and then connect the dots to the best technical solution for achieving the desired results. If CIOs have weak credibility, it is likely decisions are made for them by their superiors, peers, or subordinates.

For example, if you don't step up and demonstrate that you understand the problem and that you also have the solution, other department heads are likely to go about solving the problem themselves. Moreover, they may not involve you, so it's your job to make their problems your business. If they come up with solutions, they are most likely influenced by poor research. I have seen this go badly in almost every case, costing companies millions.

Moreover, CIOs are then responsible for delivering the results on IT projects irrespective of who makes the decision. I have seen many system implementations that failed to meet expectations because of this very phenomenon.

If IT doesn't step up, other, people will make technology decisions without the training and knowledge to do so effectively, leaving the CIO to implement an expensive bit of technology that doesn't meet the real business need.

The second aspect of technology leadership is your ability to foresee problems and devise technical solutions for things no one has seen or asked about specifically. Countless problems are hidden below the surface, so no one seeks to address them. You, as a technology leader, can bridge that divide by leading the change with new technology.

For example, in large companies, there is no one person specifically responsible for end-user productivity. Every department head focuses on their function and their metrics. However, the underlying technology, or lack thereof, for improving end user collaboration and productivity is not something they would specifically ask you for. It's not likely to show in anyone's project list. CIOs can see the hidden potential of saving energy with better collaboration tools and champion the effort to bring in the latest and greatest tools for unleashing a team's productivity.

Imagine a large user-based company operating in hundreds of functional and geographical silos, all focusing on their individual team goals but not effectively sharing information across teams. They are likely to have lots of local applications, storing all their data on local PCs or in small team folders, communicating by email at best, and so on. You, as a technology leader, could bring in a new collaboration suite that integrates all aspects of collaboration—device, information, process, and people. You could, for instance, implement a solution that integrates email, files, calendar, contacts, data repositories, messaging, audio, and video communication among all users across all their devices—PC, tablet, mobile phone, public PC, and so on.

Another example could be the use of the latest Big Data Analytics tools or the use of Blockchain technology that can change the way we do business today. These kinds of examples can be found in all other instances where it's the CIO who must take the initiative and lead the change.

Prove your entrepreneurship skills

True entrepreneurs have immensely clear vision. They may or may not have as much clarity on how to get there, but they know the endgame and are determined to reach that state. While getting to their destination, they will come across hundreds of hurdles. Similarly, CIOs who demonstrate entrepreneurial skills usually don't take no for an answer quickly.

Every step of the way, there will be lots of naysayers or excuses in the path or blocking the destination itself. Many folks may disagree with a software selection, a vendor, how long it takes to implement, the best way to implement it, and so on. The CIO's job is to always keep the endgame in mind along with business goals and using the CEO thinking cap to resolve the hurdles along the way. Obstacles may come from any direction—subordinates, peers, users, superiors, auditors, or competitors. It's the CIO's job to remove all those obstacles by building consensus and clearing the path.

Entrepreneurs are also never satisfied with the status quo. Rising above and moving beyond the status quo is an essential skill for CIOs. Most IT departments are buried in "business as usual" mode, and most of the time, teams keep doing activities precisely the same way because that's how it has been done. They don't question the status quo. Unfortunately, many of the old practices are no longer valid or as value-adding as they once were.

CIOs with entrepreneurial skills will question every process and change them along the way where necessary. For example, buying software or hardware maintenance contracts, where millions of dollars are spent without validating whether that adds value or not. As we discussed in the cost-management section, the vast majority of hardware and software maintenance contracts don't add corresponding value, but without someone questioning, IT teams are likely to renew all those contracts without even thinking twice.

Entrepreneurs are also, by definition, not averse to risks. That skill is essential for CIOs because every decision they make is based on risk assessment. Your entrepreneurial and leadership skills are critical for taking calculated risks in all aspects of running IT, whether it's related to picking software, hardware, a new architecture, or a business partner.

Entrepreneur CIOs are also very creative in figuring out solutions that are right for the company at the right price and with a high likelihood of success. Without such creativity, you are likely to do things the way they have always been done. Commonly, you will hear a project must be delayed due to lack of resources, money, user support, or something like that. CIOs with the right entrepreneurial skills will go one level below to understand the real root cause. It is almost always something you can work around.

Understand that it's people who succeed or fail, not technologies

It is of utmost importance that CIOs understand the real factors for the success or failure of any IT initiatives. It's not the technology or specific software or hardware that fails. It's almost certainly the people behind it, whether it's due to poor judgment or misalignment during the evaluation, implementation, or post-implementation of any solution.

You will see a long list of reasons why projects fail but very rarely will that list show that it's people skills or capabilities that are the culprit. You would then wonder how that technology succeeded for a competitor. It's because it's not the technology but how people use it. I have seen many cases where a chosen solution had no direct connection to the issue at hand, but technology looked so promising that someone had to have it.

You have to take extra steps to detect whether the issue is technical or human related. That detection and then acceptance is the most crucial step in solving the real problem. Once you realize the project can be salvaged by making some changes that may not be related to technology itself, addressing those take people and leadership skills, not technical skills. For example, there may be a misalignment between the team members, roles and responsibilities may not match their skills, the experience level may be inadequate, or leaders have not provided a clear direction, and so on. None of these issues are technical but purely human resource management opportunities to turn around the situation from failure to a success.

Know your audience in every interaction

Clear communication is an essential CIO skill. You must be able to speak to users in pure business terms and talk to IT teams in technology terms. The key to understanding this communication is to know your audience. You are interacting with a wide variety of people with their own perspectives, backgrounds, and technical knowledge. You are also interacting with people at different levels of management. Essentially, you must realize you are speaking in ten different languages depending upon the audience. You must tune your dialogue to the audience you are in front of.

Choosing the right business or technical terms and picking the right level of detail is very important. What could be a massive document for detailed execution in technical terms may have to be summarized in a single sentence for communicating with the CEO.

Note that a person's background dictates how they want to hear information. If you are talking to engineering or finance managers, provide precise details instead of a very high-level synopsis. At the same time, if you are working with the CEO or board members, you must summarize the plan in simple, easy-to-understand terms.

Communicating in the right language for the audience is key to establishing credibility and gaining trust. If the audience fails to understand you, especially if there is too much technical jargon, they will most likely walk away suspecting you are hiding something. The fact that we are dealing with complex technology is not an excuse for communicating with non-technical personnel with technical jargon.

Understand the technology procurement; it's really a specialized skill

As we discussed in the chapter "What Drives IT Costs Higher," technology procurement is a specialized skill. It's worth spending time learning specific dynamics at work in the IT industry instead of just relying on general experience.

I have seen many purchasing teams using standard negotiation techniques for reducing the price who, in the end walk, away with the poor deals. Realize that poor deals do not necessarily mean expensive. Usually, the undesired terms in the contract hurt you more over the long term than the price tag. The IT industry has unique dynamics, such as technology obsolescence, competition among solution providers that leads to a shorter life span for many IT companies, structural industry shifts (Cloud), and availability of new technologies. These factors make technology procurement very challenging.

Many leading industry organizations provide special training in IT procurement. They can help you understand the industry dynamics, the common pitfalls in IT procurement process, how to understand and define technology contracts, the best approach for working with IT vendors, and so on.

Depending upon the size of your annual budgets, effectively managing your procurement process can make a big difference. As mentioned in the earlier chapter, if you can't add any other business value, the least you can do as a competent CIO is to manage IT costs well. That's your responsibility.

Market IT; it's necessary but something most IT departments are not very good at

Given the technical background of most IT leaders, marketing is an ignored area in most IT shops. However, given that it's an internal service function supporting hundreds or thousands of users, effective marketing is essential to successful IT missions.

We are not talking about hyper-marketing or advertisements as seen in commercial enterprises promoting their products or services. We are talking about effective communication, education, adoption, and training. These are all forms of marketing.

Many of these aspects are crucial for service desk operations, the frontline to the user base. Many IT departments have communications and presentations created by technical team members in technical jargon with another technical person in mind as the audience.

I see hundreds of such communication threads filled with jargon that few people outside IT would ever understand even though the terms used are basic terminology inside IT. Words such as server, router, switch, DNS, Active Directory, hostname, IP address, patching, imaging, cluster, QoS, Prod, Dev, QA, Testbed, and so on are commonly used in user communications. Few people outside IT will understand what these words mean, but many of our outbound communications are full of such jargon. The same is true for the training material. It must be simple enough, both in content and presentation, that any user can quickly grasp the concepts.

Another critical aspect of marketing is collateral branding. Having all communication materials look and feel the same and offering a consistent message goes a long way in building credibility for an internal brand.

Hiring internal marketing specialists who are good at standardizing communications, training material, user documents, flyers, tips, newsletters, or support portals is money well spent for connecting IT departments to the user base. Many of these communication and education mechanisms are now using modern, multimedia capabilities to deliver the message in different forms beyond just written documents, allowing users to grasp the concepts much better and quicker with audio and video collateral.

Know the numbers—financial management skills are a must

Given that IT cost management is one of the key three areas we discussed, every CIO must have essential financial management skills. Depending upon the size of your company, CIOs are charged with effectively managing tens to hundreds or millions of dollars in operating and capital budgets annually.

Managing that kind of spending requires specialized skills. If the CIO has a purely technical background and no formal business education such as an MBA or exposure to any other business functions, they may be ill-equipped to manage budgets of such enormous size. Understanding the basics of financial management in a business context is very important. Familiarity with income statements, balance sheets, and cash flow statements is critical for a CIO to assess the company's financial status through the eyes of shareholders. However, as an internal management member, you must be adept in all the internal managerial accounting tools such as profit and loss statements, gross margins, depreciation schedules, capital versus operating expenditures, return on assets, cost of capital, and so on.

Effective financial management means:

- Paying attention to every detail. CIOs must know where every dollar is going.
- Setting up granular budgets by appropriate levels such as departments, geographies, cost centers, and account groups that can be managed effectively by a team of managers.
- Reviewing budgets and actuals at a granular level at least monthly.
- Understanding the deviations from budgets or prior levels.
- Following such deviations, understanding the root causes, and taking corrective actions.
- Identifying significant reduction opportunities and devising projects to accomplish those.

A financial analyst with IT budget-related skills would help you not only in understanding where the money is going but also in identifying the areas with the potential for significant cost reductions. An analyst with excellent analytical skills can find the hidden patterns of where money goes and if it is spent wisely.

Like IT marketing, financial management is another crucial area often ignored in IT. At every place I have worked as CIO, having an IT-focused financial analyst and a marketing analyst are always my first and second priorities. These two roles are very helpful but are often overlooked because they are not core to IT services.

Understand the unique needs in IT Talent management

IT talent management is unique. When it comes to talent management, most other functions in the company are focused on performance management. The performance management processes most companies have are good at evaluating individuals' performances. However, IT department challenges go a step beyond performance management. In IT, by the time you are proficient in any given skill, it is obsolete; turnover is high due to high demand, and labor costs fluctuate wildly based on supply and demand. This, in turn, creates capacity issues where some skills are in excess while some skills have an acute shortage.

The best way to manage these two challenges of skills and capacity mismatch is by establishing an annual process for evaluating associate's skills and determining whether they match today's needs.

For example, if you have outstanding developers in older client-server technologies and they are not able to adapt to newer mobile or web technologies, you will find that you have a surplus of one type and a shortage of another skill. The same is true on the hardware side as skills needed to manage physical servers may not be quickly shifted toward managing virtual servers unless adequately trained. Another example would be the transition from on-premise to the Cloud. You may soon find that the people needed to take care of your on-premise environment may not have enough work if all of that is transitioned to the Cloud.

Here is another example: Most companies have had email environments on their premises with multiple Microsoft Exchange or Lotus Notes servers spread around geographically. However, more recently, most of them are getting that service in the Cloud using either MS Office 365 or Google. Naturally, all the hardware and software system administrators you had for managing on-premise servers don't have to perform those tasks anymore. All those tasks are now taken over by the Cloud provider.

Good IT associates adept at learning new things are always going to be the ones you find in the top tier of your high-value list. However, not everyone is eager to or able to stay current, so they may end up being unable to contribute meaningfully.

Evaluating skills and capacity analysis is something that must be done at least annually. Of course, the key is to take action to correct the mismatch situations by retraining the workforce for new skills, if feasible. You may find many opportunities to eliminate legacy roles and retrain staff to work with the current environment's newer technologies. Continuous skill development is something that must be institutionalized as a core process in IT.

Realize execution is the only thing that matters when it comes to operational excellence

Every CIO must have sound operations management skills to be effective. At the end of the day, you must ensure the uninterrupted delivery of service. Consequently, there are two critical aspects of operational excellence: effective execution of IT projects and effective management of IT service delivery operations. Both are key to success. Although similar in nature, these two require slightly different operational skills.

Project Execution—Vision, talk, and presentations are good, but what matters is successfully completing projects. IT projects are full of uncertainties related to software capabilities, team capabilities, user expectations, resources, budgets, partner capabilities, the scope of the project, or some other factors. The result can be missed expectations and not so happy personnel.

Practical project management skills, along with risk, expectation, resource, and scope management are critical to successfully delivering IT projects. Typically, IT project success is measured objectively in terms of the schedule and budgets, but you could have a seriously flawed end result even if you meet budgets and timelines. In the end, if the solution does not deliver the results expected, it would still be put in the failed effort bucket.

IT teams often employ certified project managers. However, that does not ensure project success, good communication, reasonable expectations, or value. That's where the CIO's effective operations management skills come into the picture. CIOs must ensure all those things that project managers and project teams may not be able to see correctly.

Service operations—Running IT is similar to running a manufacturing operation. You have a sequence of processes that work in concert to ultimately deliver the service to end users. Yes, there are lots of specialized skills behind the scenes in infrastructure, applications, and help desk, but in the end, they all need to work in concert toward the ultimate goal of delivering services smoothly.

All routine services—Ensuring 100 percent availability of infrastructure or fulfilling end-user requests for computers or working on tickets to address the user's problems require a disciplined approach to managing effectively. CIOs must put on the hat of a factory floor operations supervisor to ensure all these sub-services are operating as designed every day.

In this aspect of operations management, what matters is running the IT shop with metrics and accountability. You must continually monitor all the critical metrics for service delivery, incident response, request fulfillment, customer satisfaction, system uptime, infrastructure reliability and availability, and so on. If you try to run the IT business without a set of defined metrics, you will have a lot of ad-hoc services operations. The only way to run a smooth operation is with standard metrics, close monitoring of deviations, and taking immediate corrective actions to prevent future deviations.

Recognize that you are a risk manager as well

Since we devoted one full section of this book toward risk management, it is obviously an integral part of any CIO's job and another essential skill CIOs must demonstrate. Understanding all the statutory regulations and company obligations from an IT perspective is part of your responsibility. Additionally, understanding all the other risk factors, such as natural disasters or cybersecurity, is equally important.

Being effective in all other areas of IT but ignoring risk management won't serve you or your company. In some respects, especially when disaster strikes, risk management skills are all that matter for a CIO's success.

In this regard, also having prior experience is not good enough. CIOs must devote a good chunk of their time to learning new risks arising from ever-evolving cyber threats or changing regulations worldwide. You must be disciplined enough to seek formal continuous learning to stay up to date on the latest risks and mitigation strategies. I can honestly say that risk management is one area where I am always learning. I don't anticipate ever stopping that learning process.

Understand the software compliance and audits

Understanding software compliance and audits is another specific skill we discussed in the context of managing unplanned costs in the chapter discussing "What Drives IT Costs Higher?" in the Cost Equation section. Software contracts are very complex, and most of the licensing terms are only codified within the contracts, not hardcoded into the software itself. Most software will work on as many machines as you install it on. This makes it all too easy to breach the terms of the contract, which is expensive when you get audited.

Software vendors retain the right to audit your use of their products. This protects their investment. Under the circumstances, software vendors are unlikely to add hardcoded controls to software any time soon.

The responsibility for ensuring continuous compliance is the customer's, and therefore, the CIO's. If you are fully compliant, there is nothing to worry about. However, since software contracts are so complex, it is very likely you will need to handle an issue or two. In the costs management section related to this topic, we discussed both the preventative as well as reactive measures that CIOs must master. Preventative measures of effective asset management with a formal process to ensure continuous compliance would, in essence, ensure easy handling of any audits that may come your way.

In summary, all these key skills and traits we discussed in this section are essential in delivering the best quality IT services. As you may have realized by now, most of these skills are generic in nature, and one doesn't need to go for any special training to acquire these skills. However, the attempt here was to illustrate the application and relevance of these traits in an IT management context and also elaborate on some skills that make a big difference. Most CIOs I know, as well as most IT associates I have worked with, possess the bulk of these skills, but this discussion hopefully improves their awareness in the context of effective IT management.

A Final Note

Congratulations! Now that you have read this book, let's talk about where you go from here. As I indicated in the introduction, this book was written with a certain audience in mind—IT professionals who want to pursue their careers and reach top spots as CIOs. However, as you might have realized, this content is useful for all IT professionals, even if they are not necessarily pursuing becoming a CIO someday.

So depending upon where you are in your career, you may set different goals for this journey. If you are a new fresh graduate wanting to build your career in IT, what got you in the door are your technical skills. So for someone like that, all the content in this book is going to be new, and you may want to start focusing on the value-creation aspects of your role as we discussed in the first section. However, if you are a seasoned IT manager and already familiar with most of the IT management concepts discussed here, you may just focus on fine-tuning your skills with this new perspective.

The key next step is to focus on actions you should pursue if you are serious about this journey. Knowledge is good, but actions are what deliver the results. Do your own quick assessment and determine which areas may have opportunities for improvement for you. It may be IT-business alignment, risk management, cybersecurity management, or one of the cost management areas. Whatever they may be, make a list of the top five focus areas you would like to focus on.

Once you establish your top five focus areas, use the relevant sections in this book to understand how your current approach differs from what we discussed here. Make a list of three to five subtle changes you would like to pursue for each of those focus areas. Experiment with those for three months and see the positive effect it will have on your performance.

This book was focused on all the non-technical aspects of the CIO job. It was focused heavily on the management aspects of the job that are crucial for your success as a CIO. Remember, as you climb the career ladder, your domain technical skills aren't good enough, so you have to start developing management skills. By the time you reach that top spot, the management skills we discussed here matter the most.

For CIOs, the challenge is to figure out how to maximize the business value while lowering your costs without taking any undue risks. If you keep this framework in mind, it will provide greater clarity for every action you pursue and every decision you make. We devoted the first section of this book to defining what business value is, why it matters, who determines it, and, most importantly, how to capture it for a successful business partnership. We also discussed all the key stakeholders and their expectations from IT departments. This section, by itself, should help you significantly improve your effectiveness in delivering your results.

If you are a mid to senior level IT manager, then you are invariably involved with risk management of one or another flavor we discussed. That risk-management section should provide you better clarity on the best ways to manage all the risks under your control. Cost management is the third key aspect that we discussed, and it's something everyone at every level is involved with either directly or indirectly. We covered all the unique aspects of cost management pertaining to IT.

Now that you have read my book, I would love to hear from you. I encourage you to contact me to tell me what you liked or disliked so I can improve it in the next release. More importantly, tell me about your specific challenges with any issues we discussed here so that I can help you in whatever way I can. Please feel free to reach out to me at info@perfect-imbalance.com or at Manathkar@perfect-imbalance.com or at (480) 567 5333 or connect with me on LinkedIn at https://www.linkedin.com/in/umeshmanathkar

I wish you the best of luck in building your IT career and becoming CIO one day. I am confident that, if I can do it, you can do it too.

Sincerely,

Umesh Manathkar

APPENDIX I

Key Stakeholders and Their Expectations

Role	Key Priorities	Key IT Expectations
CEO	• Meeting financial goals • Profitable growth • Innovation to stay ahead of the curve • Long-term strategy	• No interruptions to business operations • No system-caused hindrance in achieving financial goals • Full compliance • Secure • Be a catalyst to drive innovation helping the company meet goals
CFO	• Meeting cost goals • Timely and accurate bookkeeping • Finance team burnout/efficiency • Compliance	• Lower IT costs • Hands-down support for the Close • IT and Financial compliance • No systems interruptions during the Close • Topmost priority for all Finance needs
Board of Directors	• Company Governance • Long-term strategy	• IT to play a crucial role in company growth

Role	Key Priorities	Key IT Expectations
Audit Committee	• Risk management	• Cybersecurity • Regulatory compliance • Backups and Disaster Recovery • Business Continuity
Business Unit GM	• Product line or Line of Business revenue growth • Customer engagement	• Dashboards for revenue performance • Product line management support
VP of Sales	• Revenue goals • Sales team efficiency • Sales forecasting	• Sales tools—forecasting, CRM, revenue attainment, sales rep performance • Most updated and accurate revenue/attainment information • All customer engagement systems • Ensure sales teams are focused on selling/customers and not on data prep
VP of Marketing	• Company promotion through all channels—web, print, social media	• Manage all the technology behind the scenes, while Marketing focuses on content and messaging
Chief Legal Officer	• Legal compliance • Company secretary	• Support all case and matter management needs • Litigation support/discovery support • Ensure adherence to defined (or sometimes undefined) document-retention policies
VP of R&D / CTO	• Innovation • New Product Introduction	• Ensure all R&D systems and infrastructure are always available • Ensure scientists are doing the most value-added tasks • No interruptions to product schedules due to systems

Role	Key Priorities	Key IT Expectations
VP of Mfg.	• Meet all goals for product shipments (throughput), quality, cycle time on a daily/hourly basis • Mfg. efficiency/productivity improvement • Product cost • Asset use	• All Mfg. Systems must be up 24-7 at all factories • Support all continuous improvement projects • Be the lead in driving Mfg. efficiency
VP of Supply Chain and Logistics/ Procurement	• Ensure smooth running supply chain • Reduce material cost • Production Planning	• Automate all the Planning activities (most difficult) • Help reduce product cost

Community	Key Priorities	Key Expectations
Employees/ End Users	• Perform their tasks • Be as efficient as possible	• Best in class technology (doesn't care about costs) • Latest and greatest hardware and software • No constraints. Work as freely as possible. Security is essential as long as it doesn't get in the way. • Don't add burdens
Customers	• Best-in-class product/service and cost • Best-in-class customer experience	• Make my life as easy as possible. Ease of doing business • Must work in the digital economy. Don't burden me with your technology lag
Suppliers	• Grow this account and sell as much as possible with the highest margin possible	• Make it easy for me to do business with you • Get paid on time, without having to send reminders • All interactions and transactions must be in the latest digital form

Computer Worm. A standalone malware program that replicates itself to spread to other computers. Often, it uses a computer network to spread itself, relying on security failures on the target computer to access the network.

CRM—Customer Relationship Management. A software system that companies use to manage all customer-facing engagement activities and back-end sales activities on one integrated platform. A leading example of a CRM system is Salesforce.com.

CXO—Chief X Officer. The highest-level executives in company with responsibility for a specific area such as finance, R&D, IT, marketing, and so on. This generic term refers to a group of such executives who form the C-Suite.

Cybersecurity. A field dedicated to the protection of computer systems from theft or damage especially from cyber-attacks to their hardware, software, or electronic data, as well as from disruption or misdirection of the services they provide.

Data Center. A facility used to house computer, networking, telecommunication, and storage systems. It also includes redundant backup power supplies, redundant communications connections, environmental controls (e.g., air conditioning, fire suppression), and various security devices.

Database. Specialized software designed for intelligently and efficiently organizing, storing, and accessing data electronically. It's an essential building block of all software systems.

DBA—Database Administrator. An IT professional specializing in managing database software systems used for storing and organizing data. DBAs are also typically responsible for capacity planning, installation, configuration, database design, migration, performance monitoring, security, troubleshooting, and backup and data recovery.

Dev—Development Environment. An instance of servers and software dedicated to computer programmers for software development. It's a separate instance from the production environment so that the development process does not interfere with the real system.

DevOps. A clipped compound of "development" and "operations" is a software engineering culture and practice that aims at unifying software development (Dev) and software operation (Ops). It aims to improve development cycles, deployment frequency, and quality of releases.

Developer/Programmer. Also referred to as software developer or software programmer, this person creates computer software and may be a specialist in one area of computers or a generalist who writes code for many kinds of software.

DLP—Data Loss Prevention. A set of tools and processes used to ensure that sensitive data is not lost, misused, or accessed by unauthorized users.

DMZ—Demilitarized Zone. Perimeter network that contains and exposes an organization's external-facing services to an untrusted network, such as the Internet. It functions as an isolated network positioned between the Internet and the private network and allows the organization extra time to detect and address breaches before they penetrate internal networks.

DNS—The Domain Name System. An essential component of the Internet, it provides a naming system for computers, services, or other resources connected to the Internet or a private network. It also translates simple domain names to their numerical IP addresses needed for locating and identifying computer services and devices with underlying network protocols.

DR/DRP—Disaster Recovery Plan. A documented process and procedures to recover and protect IT infrastructure in the event of a disaster. Such a plan specifies the procedures an organization is to follow in the event of a disaster.

DRM—Digital Rights Management. A systematic approach to copyright protection for digital media. It prevents unauthorized redistribution of digital media and restricts the ways consumers can copy content based on their authorization levels.

ERP—Enterprise Resource Planning. Formerly referred to as a methodology, it is now commonly used to refer to a software system that governs the company's Enterprise resource planning process. ERP software integrates areas such as planning, purchasing, inventory, sales, marketing, finance, and human resources in one system.

EULA—End User Licensing Agreement. Alternatively, software license agreement, is the contract between the licensor and purchaser, establishing the purchaser's right to use the software and the terms of use.

Functional Analyst. A type of business analyst who specializes in a specific technology, a line of business, domain, or industry. These functional analysts, owing to their expertise in a particular field, are fully aware of the attributes, characteristics, and functions of their area.

High Availability (HA). A system design that aims to improve operational performance, usually uptime, for a higher than normal period. It's often achieved by a pair of systems (hardware or software) such that if one fails, the other takes over without interrupting the service.

HIPAA—Health Insurance Portability and Accountability Act. A 1996 act of United States legislation that provides data privacy and security provisions for safeguarding medical information.

HRIS—Human Resources Information System. A specialized software system to help companies manage HR transactions and activities electronically.

ISO 27000 Series. Information security standards published jointly by the International Organization for Standardization (ISO) and the International Electrotechnical Commission (IEC).

IAM—Identity and Access Management or Identity Management. The security and business discipline that enables authorized individuals to access the needed resources at the right time and for the right reason.

IP Address—Internet Protocol Address. A numerical label assigned to each device connected to a computer network that uses the Internet Protocol for communication. An IP address serves two principal functions: host or network interface identification and location addressing.

ISP—Internet Service Provider. An organization that provides services for accessing, using, or participating in the Internet.

IT—Information Technology. A department in any organization that is responsible for managing Information Technology services.

ITaaS—Information Technology as a Service. A segment of the cloud computing industry that treats IT as a commodity, providing an organization with precisely the amount of hardware, software, and support it needs for an agreed-upon monthly fee.

ITAM—IT Asset Management. The set of business practices that join financial, contractual, and inventory functions to effectively manage the IT environment. Assets include all elements of software and hardware used in the business environment.

ITAR—International Traffic in Arms Regulations. A regulation by the United States government designed to help ensure that defense-related technology does not get into the wrong hands.

ITGC—Information Technology General Controls. Controls that apply to all systems, components, processes, and data in Information Technology (IT) environment.

ITIL—Information Technology Infrastructure Library. A leading framework widely used by IT organizations to deliver IT services. It defines a set of specific practices for IT service management that focuses on aligning IT services with the business' needs.

ITSM—Information Technology Service Management. A set of policies, processes, procedures, and metrics used by IT organizations to plan, design, and deliver IT services.

LAN—Local Area Network. A computer network that spans the organization's boundaries and connects all computers behind the firewalls separated from external networks such as the Internet.

Load Balancing. Refers to efficiently distributing the incoming load (network traffic, CPU load, transactions) across a group of hardware devices to match system capacity to the demand.

Middleware. Specialized computer software that provides services to software applications beyond those available from the operating system. It can be described as software glue.

MPLS—Multiprotocol Label Switching. A type of data-carrying technique for high-performance telecommunications networks. Typically used for connecting various offices over a high-speed, private network.

MSA—Master Services Agreement. A contract in which the parties agree to most of the terms that will govern future transactions or future agreements.

MS Exchange. A mail server and calendaring system developed by Microsoft. It runs exclusively on Windows Server operating systems.

NDA—Non-Disclosures Agreement. A legal contract between at least two parties that outlines confidential material, knowledge, or information that the parties wish to share with each other for specific purposes but want to restrict access to by third parties.

Network Switch. A computer networking device that connects devices on a network by using packet switching to receive, process, and forward data to the destination device.

NIST 800. A series of documents that describe United States federal government computer security policies, procedures, and guidelines set by NIST (National Institute of Standards and Technology), a unit of the Commerce Department.

Office 365. An email service by Microsoft in the Cloud. Used by many companies as their email system.

OSHA—The Occupational Safety and Health Administration. An agency of the United States Department of Labor established under the Occupational Safety and Health Act. OSHA's mission is to "assure safe and healthy working conditions for working men and women by setting and enforcing standards and by providing training, outreach, education, and assistance."

PaaS—Platform as a Service. A segment of the cloud computing industry focusing on services that provide a platform for customers to develop, run, and manage applications without the complexity of building and maintaining the infrastructure themselves.

Patch. A set of changes to a computer program designed to update, fix, or improve it. This includes fixing security vulnerabilities and other bugs, with such patches usually being called bug fixes.

PCI—Payment Card Industry. Several credit card companies formed a Security Standards Council with the goal of managing the ongoing evolution of the Payment Card Industry Data Security Standards.

POC—Proof of Concept. A functional iteration of a particular method or idea to demonstrate its feasibility, typically performed as a precursor to a major project/investment to validate the benefits before committing fully.

Prod—Production Environment. An instance of the servers/system that hosts the software that users directly interact with.

QA Environment. An instance of servers and software where you test your upgrade procedure against data, hardware, and software that closely simulate the Production Environment and where you allow intended users to check the new release of the software.

QoS—Quality of Service. An advanced feature of network circuits that prioritizes internet traffic for specific key applications, Ethernet LAN ports or specified MAC addresses over the other to minimize the impact of occupied bandwidth from less critical services.

Router. A networking device that forwards and directs the traffic of data packets between computer networks on the Internet. Data sent through the Internet, such as a web page or email, is in the form of data packets. A packet is typically forwarded from one router to another through the network of routers until it reaches its destination.

RPO—Recovery Point Objective. Refers to the allowable age of data that must be recovered from backup storage to resume normal operations if a computer, system, or network goes down because of hardware, program, or communications failure.

Glossary

BCP—Business Continuity Plan. A strategy for recognizing threats and risks to a company, with an eye to ensuring that personnel and assets are protected and able to function in the event of a disaster.

Business Analyst. Someone familiar with the business process and domain knowledge. In IT projects, serves as a business expert to understand the problem and define a solution that can then be developed by others. Usually a critical link between users and developers.

CIO—Chief Information Officer. The head of Information Technology in a given organization. Sometimes titles may differ, such as Vice President of IT or Director of IT.

CISO—Chief Information Security Officer. The highest-level cybersecurity executive in an organization responsible for establishing and maintaining the cybersecurity program to ensure information assets and technologies are adequately protected.

Cloud/Cloud Computing. A metaphor referring to a shared pool of computer systems hosted by a third party away from your premises. This may include hardware, software, data storage, or other IT components. Cloud computing relies on sharing resources to achieve coherence and economies of scale, like a public utility.

Co-location (Colo). A data center facility in which a business can rent space for servers and other computing hardware. Typically, a Colo provides the building, cooling, power, bandwidth, and physical security, while the customer provides the servers and storage.

Computer Virus. A type of malicious software that, when executed, replicates itself by modifying other computer programs and inserting its own code. When this replication succeeds, the affected areas are then said to be "infected" with a computer virus.

RTO—Recovery Time Objective. A targeted duration of time within which a business process must be restored after a disaster (or disruption) to avoid unacceptable consequences.

SaaS—Software as a Service. The most significant segment of the cloud computing industry. It's a software licensing and delivery model in which software is licensed on a subscription basis and centrally hosted.

SANS 20. Cybersecurity framework of twenty Critical Security Controls (CSC) defined by SANS Institute, a leading cybersecurity organization focusing on cyber guidelines, standards, and training.

SDWAN—Software Defined Wide Area Network. Next generation technology that allows companies to build higher-performance WANs using lower-cost and commercially available internet access, enabling businesses to replace expensive private WAN connection technologies such as MPLS.

Server—Hardware (like a PC) that is typically housed in a Data Center. It hosts a set of software or data that the company uses.

SIEM—Security Information and Event Management. Software and services that combine SIM (security information management) and SEM (security event management) functions into one security management system. They provide real-time analysis of security alerts generated by applications and network hardware.

SLA—Service Level Agreements. An agreement between a service provider (either internal or external) and the end user that defines the level of service expected from the service provider. SLAs are output-based in that their purpose is to define what the customer will receive.

SOX—The Sarbanes–Oxley Act of 2002. A United States federal law that set new or expanded requirements for all US public company boards, management, and public accounting firms.

SSO—Single-Sign-On. An access control mechanism that allows users to use a single ID and password to access multiple systems behind the scenes.

Storage. Computer data storage is specialized hardware designed for storing mass volumes of data. Typically, companies consolidate all their data to a few such devices housed in the data center along with other server hardware and other networking equipment.

Systems Analyst. A systems analyst is an IT professional who specializes in analyzing, designing, and implementing information systems. Systems analysts typically specialize in one or more systems and act as subject matter expert for that system.

TCO—Total Cost of Ownership. A financial estimate intended to help buyers determine the total direct and indirect costs of a product or system.

TEM—Telecom Expense Management. A set of tools and services that help organizations optimize and manage all telecom expenses across voice, data, and mobile services.

VoIP—Voice over Internet Protocol. The technology that enables delivering telephone calls (voice) over the Internet as the transmission medium instead of traditional PSTN lines.

WAN—Wide Area Network. A computer network with no physical boundaries, extended to any location in the world for operating within a safe network environment. Organizations use wide area networks to relay data to their users from various locations around the globe.

About the Author

Umesh Manathkar is Corporate Vice President and Chief Information Officer of Amkor Technology. Manathkar also held CIO roles at Cree Inc. (NASDAQ:CREE) and Silicon Laboratories, Inc. (NASDAQ:SLAB) in the past. Umesh is a three times recipient of "CIO of the Year" awards in Texas and North Carolina. Manathkar is recognized among his peers as a transformative IT leader. He has also spoken extensively at industry conferences. Manathkar holds a bachelor's degree in mechanical engineering, a MS in industrial engineering, and an MBA in technology. Both master's degrees are from Arizona State University.

Umesh and his wife, Smita, live in Chandler, Arizona, with their children, Rohan and Ria.

www.ingramcontent.com/pod-product-compliance
Lightning Source LLC
LaVergne TN
LVHW092008050326
832904LV00017B/318/J